signposts
to service excellence

Our destination is never a place, but rather a new way of looking at things
John Pearson, British theologian.

signposts
to service excellence

SHEPHERD SHONHIWA

University of South Africa
Pretoria

© 2001 University of South Africa
First edition, first impression

ISBN 1-86888-168-7

Published by Unisa Press
University of South Africa
PO Box 392, Unisa, 0003

Cover design and layout: Jörg Ludwig
Editor: Liz Stewart

Electronic origination by Compleat Typesetters
Printed by Interpak Books, Pietermaritzburg

contents

foreword

I am most heartened by the theme of this book, which tells the African story from the standpoint of an African who lived through the winds of change. It is not surprising that at first glance the reader will think that it is an abbreviated African history book with focus on the early 20th century. On deeper analysis it becomes clear that the background provides vital understanding of the unique characteristics of the African people which has tended to be overlooked in business situations.

This book so aptly draws educational parallels between the concept of customer service as a cultural phenomenon and practice in the prominent business enterprises around the world. That is a unique feature, which sets it apart from any customer service literature so far produced. Most fascinating is the story-telling style of analysing the successes and failures to uphold the concept of service excellence in the many fields of human endeavour. These include all the vital components of a modern nation such as business sector, political arena, quasi-government institutions, the public sector, the professions and the grass-roots community. The anecdotal presentation of real life situations encountered in all these areas so clearly orchestrates the importance of a positive service attitude.

Another inviting feature of this book is the lucid manner which, as far as possible, captures trends and practices around Africa as a continent. This lends weight to the uniqueness of Africanism, which a eurocentric writer may find difficult or impossible to fathom. Whilst this book is a simple easy-to-read material it has tremendous value to a wide cross-section of society. This embraces all citizens of our continent, especially Southern Africa, who will see their behavioural reflection in the book, non-Africans who will learn much about the special service orientation nature of African people, the student of management and commerce, who will gain much guidance, and the practising business person who should use the content as a free checklist of his or her commitment to service excellence.

African Renaissance is a new manifestation of our pride and confidence in our own continent and its constituent nations. To win that global race, service excellence must be the most prevalent fundamental exhibited by all, in all walks of life. This book is a major step in showing us some of the ways we can contribute to the nurturing of the African Renaissance.

I hope you will enjoy reading the lessons in it as I did. More than anything else, this is a book on leadership and managing change.

Cyril Ramaphosa

Chairman of Johnnic Holdings Limited, South Africa
Chairman and Chief Executive of Rebserve Limited
Chairman of Times Media Limited
Chairman of the National Empowerment Consortium, South Africa
Board Member of several South African Corporations

acknowledgements

To my wife, Francie, and children, Farai and Fungai, for sowing the seed in my mind and encouraging support through the research and writing of this book. My sincere gratitude to my personal assistant, Mutchie Dambuza, for relentless help in preparing the preliminary manuscript; my esteemed colleagues, the staff of McDonald's corporation in South Africa for initiating me to the field of service excellence and my close friend and business associate, Michael Britten, for a comfortable excursion on his luxury boat on Lake Kariba, which facilitated the tranquillity to make the final literary touches to this book.

Finally but not least, to my two parents for raising me to be a daring observer of humanity.

Shepherd O Shonhiwa

January 2000
Johannesburg

Chapter 1

Traditional African cultural scenarios

I am a proud African, born and bred in southern central Africa in a typical peasant rural environment. I hailed from these humble beginnings, for my father was not a chief, or a distant member of royalty, or an established employee at some level of any trade. These were the early 1950s and the African continent was almost a homogeneous large village characterised by the following:

- *The British, French, Portuguese, Italians, Belgians and Spanish in that order had brought about wide-scale imperialism.*
- *Nearly 100% of each nation's indigenous population was either based in rural areas or highly migrant.*
- *The economies were predominantly of subsistence level interspersed with little smokestack industries based on the agricultural natural resources.*
- *The colonising powers of the West had exerted large-scale influence on the cultural, ethical and social fabric. This was manifested in areas such as religion, education, public administration, political structures, local authorities and in social demeanour.*

TRADITIONAL POLITICAL DISPENSATION

African society had a unique political system that blended democracy with benevolent dictatorship. National identity was based on tribal groupings. For instance, the Shona tribe of Zimbabwe was the nucleus of several smaller language dialects; the Ndebele tribe was the same; the Zulu tribe in South Africa sees itself as a nation to this day, and so does the Xhosa aggregation of related tribes. The pattern is repeated throughout the continent, with some countries with large populations such as Nigeria having hundreds of tribes, such as the Ibo, Yoruba, Hausa and umpteen others. Ghana is similar on a smaller scale; Uganda has many tribes, centred on the Baganda; Zambia the Bemba, Lozi, Tonga and others; Malawi the Nyanja and Chewa; Tanzania and Kenya the Swahili, Kikuyu and many others, including those of Arabic origins. On the other hand, smaller nations such as Swaziland, Botswana and Lesotho have one main tribe with a single dominant language.

The chief was the ascribed leader of the tribe, who looked up to him for spiritual, moral and administrative guidance. Chieftainship took a linear route through one royal family based on paternal, masculine lineage. Thus it was rare, if not impossible altogether, for a tribe to be ruled by a woman. This was no indictment on the culture as being suppressive of the female species. Women were accorded a great deal of reverence and had their secure place in the home. Of course, there has been a total revolution in this mindset in the last few decades.

The chief has been introduced as a benevolent dictator, which implies automatic acceptance by the subjects. He epitomised the pride and wellbeing of his tribe through a group of elderly councillors who were in daily contact with the rank and file. As spiritual leader, he individually inspired the nation, faced no competition or threat of coup except when the lineage of chieftaincy was challenged by another family tree. He was benevolent in that he ruled within entrenched cultural parameters. While his subjects would go and work in his fields at times, the chief supported them in times of hunger and other disasters. He never set out to exploit his subjects materially or emotionally, but instead was bound by tradition to protect them at all costs. In a way this was a form of manifestation of service excellence as the chief would 'go the extra mile' to save his subjects.

This contrasts vastly with most present-day political leaders, who are in politics for self-gratification first and their followers afterwards. African populations lend themselves well to such exploitation because they still perceive a leader in the traditional mould where he was benevolent and sacrosanct.

In almost every African language the word 'opposition' is equated with the concept of enemy. This explains the hostility with which African leaders view political opponents, to the extent that almost by reflex action they stifle opposition through every means possible, including banning, imprisonment and even murder. The paradox is that societies implicitly accept the one leader/one political party syndrome. This is not surprising because that fits in with their traditional frame of reference of one chief/one tribe. Regrettably, shrewd political leaders have upheld this because it promotes their cause, but they have discarded the selfless benevolence that compels them to be indebted to their followers, including feeding them during famine.

This dichotomy is the root cause of the political turbulence that grips the continent and is manifested by tribal wars and ethnically based political parties, with the resultant rivalry culminating in coups and perpetual sabotage. The jungle rule of survival of the fittest now pervades the political landscape, with serious implications for the economic and social wellbeing of the continent. In the new society the leaders do not view their followers as customers who need to be satisfied but rather as a means to achieving their own ends.

MILESTONES OF THE AFRICAN WINDS OF CHANGE

There was a significant migration of black Africans from their countries of birth to Europe and North America in pursuit of higher education. Those from the first countries to become independent, such as Nigeria, Ghana and Burkina Faso in the west and Ethiopia in the east, took the lead in this sojourn. The majority returned to Africa after many years, but some established roots in the host countries. Inevitably they brought back a new eurocentric social and economic frame of reference as well as outlook to life. This is how the traditional African perception of the socio-economic environment was gradually diluted. The resultant clash of ideologies was

3

far-reaching both in terms of geographical coverage and endurance in timespan, which are still abundantly evident to this day.

Common examples in present-day life bear this out. Some parents charge exorbitant amounts of *lobola* (bride wealth) when their daughter gets married, although the daughter detests the practice; to some societies birth control is taboo; women's dress and social position are dictated by culture; and so forth.

The so-called generation gap has become so wide that at times parents and children are torn apart. However, it is fair to observe that some societies and individuals have managed the change better than others.

This change has given rise to double standards in that customer orientation and service excellence perceptions and relative judgements differ between the traditional African and the eurocentrically based person. Sometimes these differences are as distinct as apples and oranges. (This concept will be clarified below.)

WHICH AFRICA?

The African continent covers the entire culture-rich sub-Saharan region from the desert down to the southern tip of Cape of Good Hope in South Africa. While religions, complexions and the physical appearance of the inhabitants of this vast area differ noticeably, there are many overriding commonalties. Similarities of Africanness can be observed across the continent:

- *First, the societies are predominantly patriarchal, with emphasis on male supremacy, relegating the female species to a seemingly subservient position.*
- *Second, there is clear evidence of an authority hierarchy in each community with entrenched respect for elders. The person in leadership is there by ascribed power and cannot be challenged. He in turn blends benevolence with unitarianism in discharging leadership duties.*
- *Third, the populations are mainly rural, battling the odds of poverty, deprivation of opportunities and social degradation.*

4

- *Fourth, the peoples have basic inherent love and respect for humanity with a controlled desire for materialism. They are primarily oriented towards communalism, being part of the whole community, in contrast to brazen individualism.*

Generally, across the wide continent value systems are similar, with an emphasis on helpfulness, participation, humility, love for humanity, conciliation, spiritual gratification and consensus rather than confrontation.

THE IMPACT OF COLONISATION

The colonisation of Africa was the most important social, economic and political mega event that drastically changed the fabric of many societies on the continent.

The dominant colonial power was Britain, which had the grandiose plan of establishing the British Empire around the world. As a result it occupied the largest portion of Africa for the longest time with the resultant effect on the cultures of the inhabitants. The empire spread from Egypt, Nigeria, Ghana, Gambia and Sierra Leone in the west through East Africa to Malawi, Zambia and Zimbabwe in Central Africa, and Botswana, Lesotho, Swaziland and South Africa in Southern Africa. How did it influence the inhabitants of those countries?

The British exported a developed bureaucratic public administration system, which laid the foundation of present-day political structures. Because of this, Africa has produced some of the pre-eminent international diplomatic personalities. Among them are Boutros Boutros Ghali of Egypt, who became UN Secretary General, Kofi Anan of Ghana, who is the current UN Secretary General, Emeka Anyeuke, who is currently Secretary General of the Commonwealth, Sibusizo Dlamini, now Prime Minister of Swaziland, who became an executive of the World Bank, and Salim-Ahmed-Salim of Tanzania, who is Secretary-General of OAU.

British influence on the social fabric of the native people was far-reaching and permanent. The West African people maintained their traditional dress of long robes or shirts, but those further south willingly adopted the British mode of dress. Education and Christianity were the most potent weapons of colonialism, which attuned the minds of the natives to accept being ruled. Money became legal tender, which radically infused the sense of relative value of commodities and services that used to be shared freely in each community. This changed the value systems of the victims of the change process. The parliamentary systems of all former British colonies and protectorates were modelled along the Westminster system of Britain from the time each one gained independence. While many have since blended these with the American republican system of government and replaced the titular with executive heads of state, British influence on the judiciary systems and executive government machinery is still visible today. A similarly indelible mark can be seen in the corporate governance models which prevail in all the former Britain-based multinational corporations whose chairpersons were mostly British knighted gentry. Probably the predominant colonial influence was in the field of education. All British colonies were given the same system, based on the British public education methodology of the 1900s. Through the decades from the early 1900s to date most, if not all, of these countries still uphold Cambridge University examinations at Ordinary and Advanced levels, whose external examiners reside in Britain. What has been the effect on service excellence of this myriad of events across Africa?

The fact that the education system was generally similar had profound influence on the academic and mental behavioural modelling of the various societies across the continent. This created a broadly similar platform for measuring standards of delivery in educational and social issues. In the 1930s and onwards social leaders such as politicians, doctors and educationalists from Southern Africa were already traversing to North Africa and the United Kingdom to seek higher education. Hence leaders like the late Kamuzu Banda learned medicine in Britain; the late Julius Nyerere also studied in Britain; and Robert Mugabe of Zimbabwe trained as an educationalist in Ghana and began his political career there. These and many other historical influences created a common pan-African value system of measuring what is adequate or not and right or wrong. In so far as that represented a paradigm shift from parochial to a mega-African society, one can correctly conclude that it created a new and different value system in that vast portion of Africa.

SMALLER COLONIAL POWERS

We have discussed the influence of Britain as the largest colonial power of the nineteenth and twentieth centuries. For brevity, the smaller colonial powers such as Italy, Spain, Germany, France and Portugal will be discussed simultaneously in this section. They also imposed social and political systems that influenced the social fabric of the societies they occupied. France colonised parts of North-west and Central Africa. Its influence can be seen today in the architecture of the main cities, the mode of dress, and social patterns of the people of those countries. A prominent feature is the way in which the interface of French and African cultures has produced world-class musicians such as Pepe Kale, Kanda Bongoman, Mbilia Bell, Tabu Ley and many others from Congo, Senegal and Côte d'Ivoire. The majority of them repatriated to French cities, where they were easily assimilated because of the influence of French culture on their societies.

In the broader scheme of the scramble for Africa, nations like Germany, Italy, Spain and Portugal can be considered small colonisers. Their occupancy tenure, and consequently cultural penetration, was not as long and deep as that of Britain. Italy only had small interests in the Horn and north of Africa. Spain and Belgium shared short-term interests in Central Africa and Germany occupied South West Africa, which was later taken over by apartheid-ruled South Africa and degenerated into a battlefield in the 1970s. Portugal exerted a fair amount of influence over present-day Mozambique and Angola. The remnants of its colonisation are still evident

7

in the culture, work ethic, official language (Portuguese) and architecture of the cities in those countries. The Portuguese imbued the local people with the trading and artisan skills for which they are highly regarded in the region. Another area of influence was in economic life, where you find Mozambicans and Angolans have adopted the Portuguese work ethic of a long day starting early, with an extensive lunch break from 12 noon to 2 pm, and finishing late. The long lunch break was introduced by the Portuguese to allow for siesta because of the hot and humid climate to which they were subjected in their home country. Similarly, cooking and eating habits have been permanently transferred to native societies. Once again what does this hold for the service excellence theme?

The colonial influence tampered with the traditional cultures of those African societies, creating fragmented value systems against which service standards are measured. The once-homogeneous broader African traditional culture has become a heterogeneous landscape of societies whose common thread is Africanism. The need for revival of cultural similarity but accommodating modern evolutionary influences gives credence to the now-much-heralded African Renaissance. It is a bid for the restitution of service excellence for Africans to Africans by Africans.

Throughout the last century the influence of various colonial powers has crystallised into clear socio-economic manifestations across the continent. East Africa can be seen as the region of traders because of the influence of Dutch, Portuguese and Spanish sailors, who linked the east coast with Indians and Arabs. Central Africa became an agrarian society because of the emphasis of the early foreign powers, while Southern Africa became the region of miners owing to the nineteenth-century scramble for gold and diamonds in South Africa, Botswana, Zimbabwe and Angola. Agrarians are the food providers, traders are the middlemen and miners unlock the mineral wealth. This forms a complete value chain of service at the macro society level peculiar to Africa. The extent of urbanisation, social and political transformation became proportionately related to these mega trends.

To identify with the new civilisation, children were given names from the colonising Western languages and religious denominations. This was a complete departure from the generation of my parents, who had typically meaningful vernacular language names.

Thus apart from the impact of the occupation of the great continent of Africa in the second half of the nineteenth century the greatest socio-economic change occurred in the two decades of the 1950s and 1960s. These were manifested by:

- *political reclamation of national sovereignty on the lines of eurocentric democracy, ie adult suffrage voting rights*
- *emerging African professional and middle classes*
- *massive rural to urban migration in search of employment. This gave rise to a new society, which created the elite evident in every walk of life today.*

PHENOMENON OF THE NEW AFRICAN

We have scratched only the surface of the richness of Africanism, but space prohibits a more exhaustive discourse of the subject. Let's build on the logic of the cultural, social and economic upheaval brought about by the scramble for Africa or colonisation. In a nutshell, two worlds collided and produced a certain cross-breed society in Africa. This is the society that now determines the destiny of Africa in politics, economic reform and developing a culture of service excellence. We are at a crossroads where a great deal of impetus is required to influence trends in a particular direction.

Here is a thumb-nail sketch of the new African in no order of preference on my part. When the black Africans of the fifties and sixties ventured to the West (and a few to the East), they either returned or stayed there. Those who returned either came back with mental baggage, which used the Western frame of reference as a guiding principle in life, or they married into that culture, which assured a permanent psycho-social change.

EMERGENCE OF THE NEW AFRICAN

The emergence of the new African was more circumstantial than the result of a calculated social plan. The major driving force was the quest for political change which started around the continent in the 1940s and persisted until the mid-1990s, when South Africa became the last country on the continent to be politically liberated. The second main driving force was sheer social evolution spurred by cultural cross-fertilisation caused by colonisation, racial interface, exposure because of travel, and the force of consolidation from disparate tribes to nations.

In South Africa some legendary names spring to mind. In the early 1950s the African National Congress produced such leaders as Chief Albert Luthuli, who became a Nobel Peace Prize winner in 1961, which put him into the international limelight. The need for defiance against apartheid laws also spurred young ANC leaders like Nelson Mandela, Walter Sisulu and Oliver Tambo to seek alliances with Indian and coloured political activists to gain critical mass. Similarly, in 1959 Robert Sobukwe became the first president of the newly formed Pan Africanist Congress (PAC) with the dream of building a new united Africa. He is famous for his proclamation that: 'World civilisation will not be complete until the African has made his full contribution.' All these people represented the emergence of a new African person destined to create and pilot change not only for him- or herself, but for the majority of society. Other new Africans came via the path of religion as trained clergymen, which made them influential community leaders. Archbishop Desmond Tutu fits well into this description as a latter key player in that sphere. There were many other South Africans who took up the role of new Africans in other areas of life such as music, the arts, journalism and the like. For example, in the early 1960s a young black journalist, Nathaniel Nakasa, left South Africa on a one-way ticket to the USA in protest against apartheid. There he joined musicians in exile such as Hugh Masekela, Mirriam Makeba and Caiphus Semenya. All these great pioneers qualify as participants in the long evolution of the new African.

In Botswana, similar torch-bearers such as Sir Seretse Khama, who married a white lady during his stay abroad, also brought new influences to their people. In Namibia such names as Toivo ya Toivo and Sam Nujoma feature prominently in that category. In Mozambique early leaders like Eduardo Modlana fit into the category of the new African, followed by protegés such as Samora Machel, who became the first president of their free country. Malawi also boasts the likes of the late Kamuzu Banda, who studied in the UK and returned home to lead his country to freedom. Congo also had leaders like Patrice Lumumba, Moice Chombe and Ben Bella, while Ghana had Kwame Nkrumah. Nigeria had its first statesman, Sir Abubakha Tafewa Balewa, who led the change movement in the late 1950s. Tanzania had the late Julius Nyerere. Kenya had the late Mze Jomo Kenyatta and Tom Mboya. Zimbabwe had trade unionists of the calibre of Charles Mzingeli and politicians like Hebert Chitepo, Joshua Nkomo, Ndabaningi Sithole and Robert Mugabe.

Why are all these people important and many others before them from different walks of life? They influenced their societies' way of thinking and responding to the demands of that time to enable them to cope with the stress of change. In that sense, the new African was a catalyst of change from the traditional mould to the new world. These forces continue to carve out various destinies of our societies across the whole continent. The motivation and determination of these pioneering personalities is the hallmark of service excellence in a non-commercial sense. It was at great personal risk, loss of freedom and forfeiture of the leisurely indulgences of their contemporary folks that they chose to chart out a new course of events. They put themselves last and their society first, sometimes enduring irreparable damage to their lives through imprisonment, torture, intimidation and, in many cases, their own deaths and those of their loved ones. What causes such selflessness and courage?

Irrespective of their field of endeavour, those who contributed to the emergence of the new African were social visionaries and champions who dared to dream of something different. They were foolhardy change agents who could not be deterred by the obvious. They were trailblazers who created a new order of things and led others to follow. They created an audience of customers and dedicated themselves to serving them, almost for no direct return benefit.

MUDDYING THE WATERS

The new African was a social accident that derailed the serenity of colonisation of Africa. In many instances, a new crossroads society was born which emulated the colonial masters' culture and social demeanour to a considerable extent but still espoused the African roots. This caused confusion and stirred the mud in already disturbed social waters. Urbanisation was the catalyst that attracted tribespeople to new centres with completely new rules of living. The newcomers dressed in the manner of the colonial masters, a white shirt, suit, tie and hat for the anglophone societies and so forth. Despite short African hair they even emulated the parted hairstyle of the white man and ladies copied the fashion of large brimmed floral sunhats. Mimicking went beyond this to include social habits such as drinking tea and clear beer, entertaining a scholarly attitude that created most of the intellectuals cited earlier, and playing Western musical instruments which spurred the burgeoning music industry.

Instead of complete absorption of the various African cultures into the colonial strongholds, a new intermediate African society was created that could challenge the dictates of the colonial cultures. They endeavoured to be as self-sufficient as possible in their demarcated social settings through arts, music, entertainment and spiritual indulgence.

SECOND-GENERATION AFRICAN SOCIETY

As Africa became the melting pot of politics because of colonisation (also notoriously dubbed political rape) much further-reaching fundamental fusion took place at social level. Both by agreement and economic compulsion white settlers cohabited with African natives of the opposite sex. In some cases it was the white employer who coerced his or her black employee into a sexual relationship. Yet in other cases parties from across the colour line did this by consent, a trend which continues today among couples from different racial groups. These unions produced the so-called coloured African, who is slightly lighter in skin colour than the native African. For purposes of this discussion this category will be referred to as the second-generation Africans. There are larger concentrations in those regions where there were large contingencies of settlers such as South Africa because of the gold rush and East Africa because of the influx of traders of Arabic and Portuguese origin. Consequently, this society sometimes took a middle of the road culture, borrowing from both sides of its biological extraction. In later years of political development across the continent this group was exploited by the colonial political structures since members of the group were not seen as white enough to belong to the privileged society. In deeply discriminatory societies such as pre-1994 apartheid South Africa they were mainly classified as native Africans, although sometimes accorded one step better. In places such as Zimbabwe, East and Central Africa, where racism was not as irrevocably entrenched by law, this group was clearly the halfway point between two racial poles. How did this influence this grouping?

In many ways they felt social and economic deprivation because of disenfranchisement in the same way as the natives. Consequently they struggled for survival in a similar fashion. Some are now fourth or fifth generation in Africa and can only refer to this soil as their true home. Their personality and cultural reflexes originate from the African context.

The second significant twilight society in sub-Saharan Africa is the Indian community. It is predominant in South Africa, East Africa, Central and Southern Africa, in that order. This is a society of commercial traders, who play a major role in the formal business sector, particularly the retail and wholesale sectors. They also produce fine doctors and accountants for the professional sector. Their origin in Africa dates back to the nineteenth century, when they were conscripted to work on sugar cane fields on the east coast of South Africa or voluntarily left India to trade in Africa. The strong bond between this society and the Africans developed from the time of Mahatma Ghandi, the great passive resistance Indian leader, who began his defiance of white oppression in South Africa. His selfless sacrifice was of major inspirational value to African political leaders as well as the rank and file. In the fullness of time Indians became integrated with other African people in the region in one large heterogeneous society called the black community, which fought for the same rights and democratic status in many countries in Africa.

The invaluable contribution of Indians to the commercial sector was amplified in Uganda in the 1970s when dictator Idi Amin expelled Indians from the country. Their exodus dealt an indelible blow to the economy, from which it still has not fully recovered over 30 years later. Thus, in their own way Indian Africans are service champions of note who have played this role for several generations, and which has won them their de facto place on the continent. Because of their keenness to trade with any customer who walks into their business place, they have earned the affectionate nickname in central Africa of *Buya tikapangana* which means 'Come in, let's negotiate even if you do not have enough money.' This is surely the epitome of service excellence behaviour.

THE UNIQUE AFRICAN SITUATION

Having described the African in the context of this book, let us see what makes this group special in any way. First, the economic history of the African continent is common. The colonisation of Africa was motivated primarily by economic imperatives and secondarily by the need for political domination. Invariably countries on the continent served as suppliers of raw materials to their Western power from agricultural, mining or marine resources. This should be viewed against the abundance of mineral wealth of the continent, ranging from gold, nickel, platinum, chrome, asbestos, copper, tin, iron, zinc to oil and many others.

With its burgeoning population, Africa has always been a lucrative market for goods manufactured in the west and east of the globe. When I grew up in a former British colony in the 1960s, every commodity had the inscription 'Made in England', whether it was a mineral or agricultural item. In hindsight, I am almost certain these finished goods were only the end result of a beneficiation process of raw materials from Africa (probably the same country) which came back to be resold as finished goods.

WHY ALL THIS HISTORY?

First, working definitions of the major concepts of our discussion would help. The term 'customer' is used in a broad sense to denote any person or group of people who receive, or expect to receive, or are entitled to a service, from an individual or institution. Service excellence means the dispensing of service beyond the standard or level generally expected by the recipients. Service excellence should make the recipient say: 'WOW – I did not expect it to be that good.'

Does society require or expect certain minimum levels of service from various providers such as business houses, public offices and other institutions? The answer is 'yes', otherwise the phrase 'customer service' would not be so much in vogue and litigation for non-performance of contractual obligations would not be so commonplace. Therefore, service standards are important to prevent exploitation of the ignorance of those unaware of their rights by those who know.

Perception of service is relative to the prevailing circumstances and the parties involved. Like beauty, it is in the eye of the beholder. When I grew up in the rural area where a fridge, let alone electricity, was non-existent, the village storeowner sold us fizzy drinks straight from the shelf. Every one of us enjoyed them without any gripe that they were not chilled. If the same man did it today in the abundance of coolers, this would be labelled very poor service.

In the same vein, perceptions of service standards differ between eurocentrically and afrocentrically oriented people. The former are using a frame of reference of precision as a product of the high pressure society that demands it. They have been socialised from the cradle to observe that discipline which started with the mother using a cooking timer in the kitchen, progressed to the school bus which arrived within five minutes of the timetable, and was emphasised every day by a clock-watching society around them as adults. On the other hand, their afrocentric counterparts inculcated a socialisation process of a different nature. In the olden days the day was distinguished by four periods, namely very early in the morning, late morning, afternoon and night. If you invited someone to come to your house for a function in the morning, they could come at 6 am or just before 12 noon because it is all morning. While industrialisation and urbanisation have gone a long way towards instilling a eurocentric perception, some customs die hard. The moral of these two parallels is that different people will use different yardsticks to measure the same situation, and of necessity will obtain different answers. This vindicates the assertion that human beings are full products of their cultural and social milieux. Each person's value system determines his or her judgement of right or wrong and good or bad. Service excellence should be seen in the light that it is only as good as the value system against which it is measured. This is of far-reaching consequence in various societies since rules and regulations of service are conceived and upheld to satisfy a particular value system.

In these circumstances how do we arrive at a universally accepted yardstick of service excellence for both those from the West and from Africa? Much of the answer lies in reducing the perceptual gap and ethnocentrism between cultures through information exchange and exposure. To this end, there is merit in the view that good customer service is a team effort, irrespective of the standpoint from which you look at it. For instance, if you went into a store with five staff and experienced pathetic service from three of them, but received marvellous treatment from the till operator and the packer at the end, did you rate that store as marvellous in customer service? In all likelihood you would rank it as low as the bad treatment given by the other three staff. This is the power of the team in upholding or destroying good service.

The complex history of contemporary African society has been outlined in order to shed light on the value systems, different cultures and economic influences which impact on customer service. It is helpful for one standing on a different side of the cultural line to understand the value system of the other in order to correctly judge the good and the bad. But each of us sees ourselves and our surroundings as the best and only mirror to model others. Therefore all forms of training and exposure to different people help tremendously in building a common frame of reference which facilitates similar evaluation of behaviour.

SELF-FULFILLING PROPHECY

Theory preaches that service excellence can be learned by any willing mind. This means there are good chances of people exceeding the expectations of those receiving their service in every activity, yet this is far from the case in our everyday experiences. Is this because of some deep-seated negativism in our society or some other inexplicable cause? The latter is not the answer but a syndrome of variables embracing culture, socio-economic influences, conflict of ideologies and non-uniformity of the benchmark standard of customer service.

In the late 1960s I was a young man who loved wearing caps. I accompanied my father to Harare in Zimbabwe, some 170 km from our farm. He wanted to buy a good business suit for which he had painstakingly saved. His mental model of the city was a product of the 1920s when whites were establishing it and there was strict separate development from blacks. Blacks had to take off their hats when in the presence of whites and they could not buy from the same stores. My father went into one of these exclusive stores because it stocked the quality of suit he wanted. As we walked into the shop my father, clearly by reflex action, took off his hat, but I kept my cap on. A white salesperson asked my father to tell me to take it off and I refused. Then he asked me directly in a half-baked language, which was only used for those ignorant of English. Little did he imagine that I was an A-grade English student in high school at the time. I answered fluently and emphatically explaining that a store was a public place and that I did not see the connection between my cap and my father's intended purchase. He turned to my father and told him he had a cheeky son.

I immediately realised that my world and my father's had collided and decided to rescue him from a predicament, like a well-mannered boy. Instead I went out of the store while he did his purchase, which he speeded up notably. On my part, I never went into that shop again for the ensuing 25 years that it existed. This shows how double standards, particularly when predicated upon racial prejudice, can completely distort the spirit of customer service.

Two friends of mine in Cape Town, South Africa, connived to undertake some investigative adventure into the customer service orientation of a leading clothing store a few years ago. One went in with unkempt hair, sandals and not so tidy clothes. He walked through the double doors where attendants wait to escort customers around and induce them to buy stacks of goods. No one paid attention to him and he wandered around the shelves alone except for one uninterested sales attendant, who kept some paces away to watch in case the prowler pilfered some items.

The second man walked in looking really high powered and well dressed. As soon as he walked in, he was mobbed by two attendants only too keen to serve him. He enjoyed the flattery for a while before it became apparent that he was not a serious buyer. The truth is the first entrant was far better endowed with money than his counterpart.

What are the lessons from this? First, there is evidence that differential treatment is accorded to customers in line with their perceived social status. Status is portrayed by your attire at that time, or the car that you parked in front of the shop, or the language you speak, or your skin colour, and so on.

In this same vein, many of my age group recall some incidents, before our African countries gained political independence from their colonial powers, when you could be stopped by a policeman if you were driving a new and expensive car, to be asked the question 'Which *baas* owns this car?' (*Baas* was the term by which every white man was called to orchestrate the master-servant relationship between the two races.)

So the second lesson to be learnt from these discourses is that the self-fulfilling prophecy phenomenon has real influence on customer service. You see what you want to see and it becomes true because your defensive ego will choose to see it like that. This therefore confirms the earlier assertion that there is no common benchmark for gauging customer service across our large and varied society in Africa. There are several nuances that come into play and distort the equilibrium of our concept of customer service.

BACK TO BASICS

Through the breadth and width of the beautiful continent of Africa there is abundant evidence of how the culture is naturally predisposed towards giving service to other people. The humility of African culture lends itself to dispensing service. There is inherent politeness and forgiveness in their interpersonal relations. Sometimes this has erroneously been perceived as a weakness by those unfamiliar with our cultural roots. Respect is an integral part of an African from the cradle to the grave. A young person does not stand in front of elders so that he or she does not look at the top of their heads. This inborn reflex comes into play in dealings with customers in all circumstances. It is also seen as being rude or threatening to persistently look straight into the eyes of another person. On the other hand, the eurocentric culture encourages eye contact as evidence of engaging the attention of the other person.

It is seen as a sign of mutual respect to debate and seek consensus instead of unilateral dictation. If an issue of common interest is being heard, the whole family will gather. The presenter of the matter addresses it to the youngest person, who refers it to the next in age, who does the same, until the matter reaches the oldest person in the line. The response comes through retracing the same steps. This is done to involve everyone in the deliberations regardless of age or sex. Such inclusiveness is designed to ensure that enough reflection is done by several people on the one issue. The objective is to eliminate all possibilities of reaching a wrong decision. In other words, this is teamwork in pursuit of service excellence.

The African greeting style has inherent caring in it. Most people give a three-step handshake with the right hand to show appreciation of the other person. The whole ritual of greeting is a sincere mutual exchange which is a calculated move and is not rushed as in 'Hi, how is it?' One would say 'Hallo' and pause a bit before asking 'How are you?' Sometimes the process is done through the referral process discussed earlier, if there are more than two people involved.

In most Central and Southern African Nguni-based languages, greeting emphasises acknowledgement of the worth of the other person. In Zulu one says *Sawubona* (singular) or *Sanibonani* (plural) which literally means 'I can see you are well'. This may be followed by clapping hands in unison, and invoking totem and clan names and seniority references. Almost always one would inquire about the wellbeing of the family or those left behind. In Shona (Zimbabwe language) one would ask *Mhuri dzakadiyi?* (How are the families?) This is indicative of the caring disposition of African culture.

Some societies in Africa hand a calabash cup of cold water as soon as they greet a person. The rationale is that the visitor must be thirsty, because of the high temperatures prevailing in most of Africa. Of course this practice is predominant in circumstances where the visitor would have journeyed on foot. From a customer care point of view the aim is to serve the visitor by satisfying his or her most urgent need. I recall again as a young boy that in some of the general dealer stores that we bought from (owned by Indians and Greeks) they would keep a bucket of water and a cup for thirsty customers.

Following the same line of caring, one is not allowed in traditional African culture to ask a visitor whether he or she wants food. The host just prepares food and offers to the visitor. This is done to save a stranger from declining an offer of food because of shyness, while he or she is really hungry. Surely, this is the height of caring for others.

In fact, the ultimate in African customer care is that a visitor is given the best food in the house while hosts make do with lesser delicacies. I remember vividly several incidents when I was a young child and visitors came to our house. A chicken would be cooked but I and other children would be given the less desirable parts of the chicken while the visitor had the juicy flesh. This did not hurt because we were socialised to please the visitor. In many ways this childhood teaching grows with you to become second nature.

It is fully acceptable that a stranger on a journey in a rural area can go to a home and ask for food and overnight shelter. The host considers it an honour to have been chosen and will provide for the person without expecting remuneration. In contrast to eurocentric cultures the African man was expected to walk in front of his wife and children carrying nothing but cultural weapons to defend his family in the event of encountering dangerous animals in the forest. Even in today's less traditional dispensation, in some societies the man comes out of the house before the woman to ensure there is no danger awaiting her.

MUTUAL CARING THROUGH COMMUNALISM

Communal living is manifested by congregations such as a village, kraal and other close-knit constellations in which African people live. It is not communism either by philosophy or practice. This aspect of life symbolises the height of caring imbedded in the culture. Villagism is not just a loose social phenomenon but an institution of shared protection and the general burden of living. It offers social insurance and a catchnet below which none of the members is allowed to fall.

In the Shona culture of Zimbabwe there is a social gathering called *Nhimbe* which can be loosely translated as organised groupwork. It entails a family brewing some sorghum beer and calling other village members to come and spend a day working in their field or on some other big task, while drinking beer and eating. At the end of the day when the task is finished, the evening is devoted to dancing and socialising. This is a major arrangement to share the burden of enormous tasks and take care of those who are unable to cope single-handedly.

Such a residual care infrastructure permeates the fabric of the entire society with a visible positive impact on destitution. In the rural area where I grew up my father had more cattle distributed around five or six families than in his own kraal. This was because he gave away most of the bulls to neighbours and friends who had not enough cattle of their own to tame into oxen and use to plough their fields. Normally the person would take one cow as well for milk, which eventually gave birth to several progeny over a few years. The net effect was manifold, including strong bonds of relationships and a spirit of gratitude which engenders honesty. For instance, when the real owner of the cattle died, all those with his cattle and other property would declare this at his funeral for the public and family to record. Then they would voluntarily return the cattle or renegotiate with the heir for a further loan period. In this sense, communalism served as self-insurance within the community against the vagaries of the environment.

Other institutional evidence of mutual caring is found in the extended family system, which absorbs the social deprivation even of distant relatives. If one is unemployed, the others will provide for the essentials of life. The concept is also extended to the inheritance of spouses and orphaned children by surviving brothers and sisters to prevent them becoming destitute. It was because of this cultural residual care that there were no orphanages and old-age homes in African villages.

THE BOTTOM LINE

African people are naturally predisposed towards rendering customer service excellence both individually and collectively. This is easily evident to any visitor to Africa's abundant tourist destinations. Humility and willingness to help are the essence of African culture which can only be further perfected through training programmes to instil the eurocentric dimensions.

CLOCK BUILDING VS TIME TELLING

So with all the glory of our culture having been sung in earlier pages, why do we not excel in service excellence?

It is because our culture was locked into a time-telling mode. It is a clever person who can tell time to the fraction of a second correctly without looking at a watch. He will help many who come across him but not those afar. The greater and more talented person is the one who can build a clock to enable many to tell the correct time for themselves. Thus he bequeaths a legacy of perfection. The transfer of history and behavioural code was through story telling by the fireside. The folly of no documentation is that perfection is diluted through generation gaps, technological change, cultural convergence, urbanisation and the deprivation of some of the subsistence village economies that prevail across the continent. African society is still in a time-telling mode. Concerted effort now needs to be put into adapting to the clock-building mindset with a framework of principles and standards engraved in documentation to stand the passage of time and change of key personalities to become a self-sustaining thrust of service excellence. This book is an attempt at preservation of the wealth of Africanism for the benefit of future posterity.

SERVICE EXCELLENCE FROM AFRICAN CULTURE

Having painted the backdrop of traditional African culture rich with humanism, humility, altruism and industriousness, we will now look at how this is translated into various permutations of customer service. The illustration will comprise many everyday events that have been contrived over time in various African communities. In pursuit of balanced reportage in later chapters I discuss cases of corruption and bad governance in political and business spheres around Africa which will ostensibly tarnish the African people's image. The following treatise seeks to counterbalance in advance the negative impression that may be created due to generalised perceptions by various readers.

ENTERTAINMENT INDUSTRY

Today Africa is well endowed with world-class musicians who all came from humble beginnings and were deprived of the wherewithal to start a music career. To mention a few, South Africa has music maestros of the calibre of Miriam Makeba, Caiphus Semenya, Hugh Masekela, Ray Phiri, Ladysmith Black Mambazo, Tsepho Tsola, Yvonne ChakaChaka, Brenda Fassie, the Soweto String Quartet, African Jazz Pioneers and hundreds more. These creative musicians were not motivated only by money to venture into this vital entertainment industry. More than anything else, they were propelled by love to change the lot of the masses for the better. When apartheid had made South African townships urban dormitories without the same social amenities as the white suburbs, musicians filled the void by creating their own music with hardly any musical instruments. An even more significant role of music was to build and sustain a psychological defence against the dehumanisimg effects of apartheid and unequal opportunities. In the same way as gospel music sustained African Americans through the ordeal of slavery, music was multifunctional as therapy, entertainment and a culture building effort in Africa.

Zimbabwe also produced equally venerated musicians such as Thomas Mapfumo, Oliver Mtukudzi, Johnna Sithole, Leonard Zhakata and Biggy Tembo in much the same circumstances as South Africa. These musicians composed and propagated songs which had a crucial motivational effect on the country's population during the *Chimurenga* war of liberation between 1972 and 1980. They mobilised the masses as much as the war doctrinaire did.

The East African region has become well known for the production of Kwasa Kwasa Rumba music, which originated from the early mining towns of the Zambian Copperbelt and the Congolese diamond mines. International singers such as Pepe Kale (nicknamed the Elephant of Africa), Kanda Bongoman, Mbilia Bell, Tabu Ley and scores of others are now beaming Rumba music from leading European cities for the entertainment of the whole of Africa and Europe. Similar trends are traceable with musicians originating from Kenya, Senegal, Côte d'Ivoire, Nigeria, Ghana and Central African Republic.

What is the relationship between these developments and service excellence? The answer is simply that these African men and women were motivated by the desire to satisfy the entertainment needs of their own people, and battled against the odds to provide a service to a high standard which has made them legendary.

SERVICE FOR SELF-SUFFICIENCY IN AFRICAN COMMUNITIES

Earlier we discussed the virtues of traditional African culture such as the extended family system, which admirably replaced Western residential institutions such as orphanages, old-age homes and other sanctuaries for the destitute. We now turn to similar efforts in modern African culture to highlight service efforts for one another within communities to upgrade their quality of life. Please be aware that these are only a representation of a myriad of service activities around Africa.

COMMUNITY DEVELOPMENT SERVICE

In traditional African rural life to this day the construction of infrastructures such as a house is often a community effort. A round hut of poles plastered with mud will take anything between a few days and a couple of weeks to build. The villagers will gather by invitation. First the men to go into the forest to collect poles and tree bark for fibre to use in construction. They will either carry them in groups or, in a more developed setting, they will harness oxen to draw the poles to the building site. Then, in keeping with societal division of labour, the women congregate to dig up clay from molehills and carry water from the river in clay pots on their heads to make mud for flooring and plastering. They will also go into the forest to cut grass with hand tools for thatching the roof. Men will then carry it home and erect the roof truss then thatch the house. All this is done for no direct payment with the psychological promise that each person will need such help at some point and that they will obtain from the other neighbours. The entire village network has survived for centuries on this basis and will continue to do so. This is the epitome of self-service for own development among Africans. The same spirit of selflessness is extended to tilling and planting fields, herding domesticated animals and harvesting crops.

COMMUNITY SOCIAL SERVICE

The one area where the humanity of the African really shines through is in the burial of the dead. Traditionally, it was a community effort even if the deceased was a poor and ordinary person. Every member of the community attended this very solemn and emotional occasion, and contributed to the decent burial of a fellow community member regardless of whether they liked the person or not. The same sense of responsibility has been developed into a well-organised social service to meet the challenges of modern commercial society. As towns and cities grew from former mining, trading and agricultural colonial settlements, the deprivation of Africans of social amenities became more glaring. One of the first and now most established social services is the burial society. This is a social organisation formed and run voluntarily by members of a particular community to finance the funerals of their members. All members pay a nominal membership fee regularly and an elected committee administers the money, including investing it wisely. As the cost of living continues to rise, pushing up the cost of dying unbearably, and as people are now living further away from one another than before, this has become a vital institution. In South Africa and Zimbabwe it first blossomed among migrant workers from Malawi who had to fortify themselves against the deprivation of being a minority community in a land far from home. The Malawi burial society system was so successful that it became a model for many other communities in southern Africa. This has become a flourishing industry with millions of dollars flowing through it per annum. It is a successful example of service to the people run by the people. Coincidentally, these are the basic tenets of democracy which guided the American constitution. Many other examples may be seen in the successful savings clubs, agricultural production and marketing cooperatives that flourish in many communities across the continent.

PROFIT-MAKING SELF-SERVICE

As the self-help initiatives such as these societies were growing, a parallel system of profit-making ventures also flourished in urban areas, boosted by the rural to urban exodus which began in the late nineteenth and early twentieth century in parts of Africa. This is particularly true of mining-based cities like Johannesburg in South Africa, the Copperbelt of Zambia and the Democratic Republic of Congo in Central Africa. This was the establishment of the 'shebeen', which is a private liquor selling outlet in a domestic house in the townships. You now find thousands of these outlets in African cities at various levels of prosperity. In many cases, as the black African elite move out of the townships in Johannesburg, Harare, Nairobi,

Durban, Lusaka and many other cities to the former white low-density suburbs, they miss the camaraderie of the shebeens and still go there for weekend gigs.

Apart from being social melting-pots where people of different walks of life met and enjoyed life, the shebeens were substitutes for the five-star hotels in the white side of the cities, fulfilling a real social need. But most of all, they yielded financial rewards which sustained whole families and put children through high school when parents were unemployed. In most cases, police would want to raid these outlets, confiscate the liquor and charge the owner as well as the patrons heavily for breaking the law on liquor control. However, there was always a common bond among residents whereby sentinels would send out word at the first sign of the police in that neighbourhood. The customer service in the shebeens is mostly very personal and friendly, including the provision of a beef braai when customers express the need and drinks on account to be paid at a future time.

Again communities identified an economic and social need and created a business infrastructure to satisfy that need while simultaneously creating wealth for the entrepreneur, who is a part of the community. The common thread still discernible here is the togetherness, caring, sharing and mutual helpfulness of the African culture.

LABOUR MOVEMENTS AND TRANSFORMATION SERVICE

In some situations trade unions have embarked on huge projects to promote transformation in their society by taking up economic equity. This has been driven mainly through some trade unions which have raised funds for skills development of their people, formulated social plans to alleviate poverty among their members in the event of being retrenched and raised funds to buy out former colonial owners.

The leading examples can be found in South Africa where unions such as the National Union of Mineworkers (NUM), South African Catering,

Commercial and Allied Workers Union (SACCAWU) and National Union of Metalworkers of South Africa (Numsa) have made substantial investments into going business enterprises. When democracy dawned on South Africa in April 1994, these unions immediately seized the opportunities that opened up for black economic empowerment. They created investment companies which operated completely separately from the trade union to avoid mixing membership security funds with those funds exposed to the vagaries of business investments. A number of them have created real wealth for their members through such investments when the stock market has risen and therefore multiplied their invested funds. Some consolidated into the National Empowerment Council (NEC) which, together with funding institutions, acquired controlling stake in Johnnies Industrial Corporation (Johnnic) from Anglo American Corporation in 1996, an enterprise with an asset value of over R3 billion at the time. By the close of the century this value had multiplied more than tenfold.

The fascinating story here is the dedication of trade union members who selflessly pursued the objective of sourcing funds from financial institutions. They avoided the temptation to use union membership funds and, sometimes against the will of some members who did not grasp the risk-reward relationship, persevered to form the NEC to facilitate one large investment instead of several small equity holdings. At the top of the dedicated leadership was Cyril Ramaphosa, former secretary general of the South African Trade Union Movement, former secretary general of the African National Congress and the principal negotiator for the ushering in of democratic rule in South Africa. He took up the helm of the NEC in 1996 and facilitated the deal with Anglo. Historical though it may be, this event is not the only example of self-service initiatives of Africans in South Africa and elsewhere in Africa. The lessons to be drawn regarding service excellence are that in their humble circumstances the African brethren enkindled trust in cooperating with one another to pursue a noble but gigantic goal for the betterment of a multitude of disempowered members and not only themselves. This is the hallmark of service excellence in community transformation and development setting.

Chapter 2

Business sector as trendsetters

In this context, business sector is defined as the all-encompassing entrepreneurial community ranging from small, micro to medium and large-scale enterprises including quasi-government business enterprises and multi-national corporations. Even the street corner spaza shop and flea-market stall are included because they are spurred by the same fundamental goal of profit-making.

SERVICE EXCELLENCE BENCHMARK

The fact that I am a corporate manager with more than two decades' experience obviously makes me biased towards that arena. My conviction is that much against the wishes of the idealist, this world measures success on the basis of materialism, be it cash or acquisitions from it. This applies equally to individuals, organisations and nations. Hence the perpetual love-hate relationship between the rich and poor nations of the world. If money plays such a pivotal role in shaping the world pecking order, credence ought to be given to the fundamental conditions that make it abundant. Without entering the controversial debate of development economics, I will proffer the hypothesis that those organisations and individuals operating in terms of free market forces in an openly competitive environment serve as the real benchmark for service excellence. If they do not meet the needs of their customers, they are eliminated by competition. Therefore, they have to remain excellent to survive.

'GOOD SERVICE' IS NOT GOOD ENOUGH

When someone says he or she had given good service to a customer, he or she should not feel inclined to brag about it. All that person has done is to earn his or her pay honestly by performing to an acceptable level. One gets an accolade only when one has rendered customer service excellence by going the extra mile to the extent that the customer says, 'Wow – I did not expect this.' Too often people are satisfied with good service, which leads to compromised standards. An example of 'good service not being good enough' is this incident. In the very recent past I travelled to East Africa with a business colleague. We were booked into an established inter-continental five-star hotel and arrived around suppertime. We were received by friendly front-office staff who seemed to be working hard but the queue of waiting customers never seemed to end. My associate was served first but not given his room keycard, being told the room was not ready. I was served sometime later and got my room keycard. We went to eat first and came back to collect his key two hours later. He went to his room but the electronic keycard could not open it. On reporting this to the front office, an apology was duly extended but it took the staff three trips to the room three floors up with umpteen different cards before the door could open. After spending ten hours flying including in transit waiting, this delay in getting to bed was not appreciated. Incidentally, the following evening, it happened again until a major discovery was made that the card coding was not the correct mode for a room with an adjoining one.

Service excellence is an all-round overwhelming phenomenon incorporating the time taken to serve, the quality of the product or service, the form and speed of delivery as well as the perception of value for money elicited in the customer. This is predicated upon the old adage that the customer is king. Is this still true in this day and age? The answer is an unequivocal 'Yes' and even more so because customers today have immense power to destroy a poor service provider through the many means at their disposal, led by the abundance of information technology. Thus an unhappy customer no longer just has a high nuisance value but is now an assassin to the provoking enterprise. It still remains an interesting paradox that a satisfied customer tells at most three other people about it, and then only when the subject comes up, but a dissatisfied one will voluntarily tell ten others. The multiplier effect of bad news is incredible. Let us turn to a simple example of service excellence. Three years ago I went to a restaurant specialising in Portuguese cuisine, in Johannesburg, South Africa. After dinner we were politely requested to complete a service questionnaire, which was quite simple and basic. However, since then my wife and I both receive a personal letter two weeks prior to our birthdays, containing birthday wishes and offering a discount for the birthday dinner plus a personalised cake. Each time we have tested them out and they have duly met our expectations. It is a foregone conclusion that this unexpected service gesture has converted our whole family to that restaurant.

TEN BEHAVIOURS FOR SERVICE EXCELLENCE

Service excellence has a direct cause-effect relationship with good management practices. Customer service occurs within a particular context in society which can be either highly structured, like a business firm, or a loose formal entity like a community organisation. To both situations there are common fundamentals. These entail the existence of customers or claimants for and recipients of some service or product from the organisation. Second, there ought to be leadership which defines the organisational parameters to create and deliver the requisite service or product. Third, within the organisational boundaries there must be some frontline members who dispense service and receive instant feedback from customers. Thus they have the power of information to instantly improve service levels or impair them. These frontliners are the service champions who make things happen to fulfil the mission of the organisation. (This concept will be extrapolated in the next section to emphasise the profit-making business entity as the pivotal instrument of creating wealth in free enterprise societies.)

Business management is neither rocket science nor a mysterious back-to-the-future whirlwind. It is all about people, as customers, as employees,

33

as relevant key publics, or as management. If you understand people, together with the forces at play in all these various categories and you are able to blend them into an equilibrium of strategic fit, you are more than halfway to best practice management. Expanding on the philosophy of people skills as the bedrock of service excellence, let us share the critical behaviours to be inculcated in each person who is in a service capacity directly or otherwise. These were adapted from Jan Carlzon (1987).

1   *Every service person must always have the big picture of the cause-effect relationship of his or her actions. It is important to start every transaction with the end in mind. This will guide his or her behaviour in handling the situation and all its ramifications. Experience has shown that staff who have knowledge of the desired outcome of their contribution serve customers better.*

2   *Understand the needs of the customer and communicate effectively with them. Knowledge is different from understanding. It could even be a self-centred definition of what you perceive as needs which may not be the correct ones. Many people are so oriented towards sales that they try to force the customer to buy what they happen to sell, irrespective of whether it meets the customer's needs or not. The preferred service hero must have a marketing orientation that dictates that the customer's needs must be identified first and effort concentrated on satisfying them.*

3   *Customer-care people must have and always display a passion for service. They must be self-regulating and self-guiding to use their reflexes appropriately as each situation demands. Self-discipline is imperative to enable compliance with the fundamental written and implicit rules of customer service.*

4   *Develop a constantly learning mode to be ahead of changes in service techniques. Incremental, small improvements are no longer sufficient to cope with today's fast pace environment. Periodical quantum leaps are now the desired form of change. A proactive service provider continuously learns from the best relevant situations and people.*

5   *Always show real eagerness to make a difference for the better in every business situation. Whether you are an office cleaner, a taxi driver, a messenger, an administrator or a manager, aim to make a contribution towards improved service in every interpersonal transaction. The moment of truth is the first point of interpersonal contact between a customer and the service provider. The initial 30 seconds are critical in forming a favourable first impression by the customer. At this juncture, employees, irrespective of level of seniority in the organisation, are the de facto representatives of their organisation. They cannot pass the buck to blame the company for poor service. There is never a later chance to make a lasting impression. This is the point where the rubber meets the road. If not well handled, the friction can be most damaging.*

6   *Many products today are very similar either in performance or features, as a result of convergence of production technology. Therefore, the main differentiation is value adding through service and quality. All employees must possess these value-adding skills and be empowered to employ them at all times. Thus, the rigid structures of the past which curtailed creativity in staff are contrary to the philosophy of service excellence. Sales people continue to sell products while customers want to buy relationships.*

7   *The spirit of serving others demands real inherent respect for other people. You cannot render excellent service to a person to whom you have a condescending attitude. You must serve because you derive absolute pleasure from it and not just money. Needless to say there is no room for racism or prejudice in service excellence. There is no end to the road to quality and service.*

8   *Break out of the traditional service mould. Shake off the stereotypes and prejudices based on history that dictate only a certain way of doing things. Service excellence comes from mavericks who defy tradition to do things differently. Tradition must be vigorously challenged constantly to promote a new way of doing things. You cannot dispense service excellence while you are a slave to a precedent set in the last century.*

9   Consistency and perseverance make a most potent cocktail for service excellence. The concept of guerrilla marketing advocates that in pursuit of service excellence you do not leave a stone unturned. Consistent effort creates a critical mass of desired customer care which ultimately breeds favourable perception by outsiders. Devoted providers of service should use this to maintain their leading edge among competition. Recipients of service are more comfortable when they can expect exactly the same service from the same source all the time.

10   Compete with yourself. Know the real standards of poor, good and excellent service. Set your standards, benchmarking with the best practices and reach for them relentlessly. It is foolhardy to compete with mediocre standards which you invariably exceed without much effort. Your inner self must be the principal driver for your success. It is often said that business is very much like tennis – those who don't serve well end up losing.

CONSCIOUS SABOTEURS OF SERVICE EXCELLENCE

Every day we witness less-than-perfect service incidents perpetrated by staff who are either aware of their failure or not trained to know better. Some examples illustrate this point. A year ago my family were on an afternoon excursion at one of the entertainment centres in Johannesburg which has many food outlets. My wife went to a fast-food outlet to buy a packet of fried chips. After some time she returned mumbling that she will never buy from that shop again or any of their brand name. She had stood around for nearly four minutes without any one attending to her. The manager could see her clearly but chose to call one of the staff to serve her. No one came to attend to her, instead a minute later the manager said no one could serve her since it was 16h00 and shifts were changing over. This demands the following questions: Why did the manager not serve her himself? Why should customer service be suspended for shift hand-over? Did the manager and staff have any passion to serve customers or was it only a job? How many such situations have you encountered?

A second incident involves myself at another fast food outlet on the beachfront in Durban, South Africa. I stood at the counter for three minutes unattended while the 'skinhead' manager was chatting to two other skinheads about non-business talk. Being particularly unforgiving of such discourtesy I walked away disgusted and made the usual promise never to go to that place again.

The third example of lack of customer orientation involves a real estate firm operating in the city of Pretoria in South Africa. They manage the leasing of many blocks of apartments around town. One tenant had rented one of them for over a year and she had always honoured her rent obligations. On one occasion she realised after ten days of the rent being due that a very close relation to whom she had given the money to pay rent had not paid. There was no reminder from the real estate but when she went to pay she was told that she was being evicted for non-payment. Indeed she and her three young children were kicked out of the apartment. When her supervisor, a director in a government department, intervened, the real estate personnel then became remorseful and said she could stay. The affected lady had already secured alternative accommodation and her pride urged her to decline their second-thought offer. Again these customer service questions should be asked: Why did the rules suddenly change after the government director intervened? Why did the agent not contact the customer soon after the payment date had passed to remind her? Why did they resort to eviction on a single default? A multitude of answers can be suggested, including sinister motives such as racism, insensitivity to customer needs, lack of human consideration, excessive profit emphasis and so forth, ad infinitum. The general observation is how many potential customers and goodwill did the real estate lose because of this incident? In fact, this was the best way of mortgaging their business goodwill and image for a long time in future.

Another fascinating example of commercialism prevailing over customer respect relates to commuter taxis in most African cities. Passengers are generally packed like sardines and then told that the person at the back should collect all the fares from the passengers and give them to the driver. If the amount is short, the taxi does not leave until the discrepancy is made up. Is it not a paradox beyond reason that passengers come on board to catch a lift and pay for it, and instead are subjected to harassment and humiliation by the person whose wages they are paying?

Yet another incident of the carefree attitude by service staff happened to me only recently on one of the major airlines in Africa. A colleague and I were flying in business class, in which case one might expect a semblance of personal service. It took quite a long time for the stewards to serve us drinks, and it transpired that only one of the two was doing it. I recognised one steward from a continental flight with the same airline the previous week. I had not enjoyed his service for the four hours of that flight because he displayed the attitude that 'I am only here to do a job to please myself, not you'.

I did not tell my colleague about this, lest I should influence his attitude towards the steward. It soon became unnecessary anyway as the steward's behaviour vindicated my assessment. As he was taking so long to serve the drinks, my colleague, who sat on the aisle seat, took two drinks from the trolley stationed next to us. This is quite common practice during flights and stewards understand it.

When the steward eventually got to us, my colleague asked for some glasses. The man answered in a very matter-of-fact tone saying, 'You served yourself, Sir'. We responded saying 'But we were helping you'. An even more emphatic response from him was 'I am here to serve you'. At his mercy, he eventually gave us glasses but our appetite had already waned.

As if that was not enough, I later went into the toilet. Hardly a minute later the same steward banged the door shouting 'Hurry up, we are about to land'. You can imagine how embarrassed I was when I came out with all the other passengers looking at me in bewilderment. I had to fight the urge to grab him by the collar and respond to his discourteous behaviour in a similar manner.

Indeed, I wrote to the top management of the airline lodging a complaint against the individual but got no response. This is a classic example of how poor staff selection and lack of training lead to mediocre staff becoming senior members of the crucial cadres that are supposed to minister to the needs of customers. By default they may even get to management, which will institutionalise mediocrity permanently.

Many people experience such tardy treatment every day but let it go because they are victims of our culture of acceptance. Inculcation of the principles of excellent service examined earlier by members of society would eliminate this sabotage.

MASTERS OF SERVICE EXCELLENCE

Indeed there are some organisations which are torch-bearers as masters of service excellence.

Anecdote one: A few years ago I flew Qantas Airlines from Sydney in Australia to Auckland, New Zealand. Two days later I flew back with the same stewardess. Soon after take-off she came to me and mentioned in a concerned voice that I did not look as well as I had done on the outward journey. She was so right because I had a severely upset stomach. I felt so flattered, not so much that she had noticed my unwellness (which any adult can do) but that she had taken the care to remember me and show concern. I was so pleased that a couple of hours later I felt much better. What was the magic? Simply the human touch and worth that was manifested by her approach. This demonstrates that relationships count for better customer care.

Anecdote two: On another occasion I flew Singapore Airlines to the Far East for the first time. A month later I flew the same route and the same beautiful stewardess in business class knew my name as I walked in and remembered my favourite beverage including the type of wine for dinner. Indeed this left me with the 'Wow' feeling.

Anecdote three: We are all accustomed to the tradition of motor repair workshops being restricted to the daytime hours of 07h00 to 17h00. This has become increasingly challenged by the changes of preferences and demands of society. One foreign motor manufacturer in Southern Africa grabbed the bull by the horns and introduced a 24-hour service. The reasoning of the CEO was that they were going to use industries other than motor industry to determine the best-practice benchmark. Pegging your service to another member of the industry encourages acceptance of mediocre standards. Therefore the strategy was to seek world norms and then compete with those. This is a welcome novel idea, which symbolises a departure from established practices. It is such propensity to break out of the mould which creates sustainable leadership in service excellence.

Anecdote 4: My fourth delightful experience involves a firm which operates a tracking system for stolen vehicles in South Africa. They fitted that system on my car, but I was unaware of the service efficiency of the firm. As part of the vehicle security, the firm obtains your full personal details and those of your partner if you have one. On one occasion the battery of my remote control unit ran out and I opened the door manually, which set off the alarm. After getting inside, the car could not start. A few minutes later my wife phoned me to check if I was fine because the tracking firm control room had phoned her and told her that my car alarm was going off, but they could not contact me on the number they had. She gave them my mobile number and immediately after that they phoned me to check what was the problem. The gentleman was polite and concerned, starting by asking me if I was physically safe and not in danger of being robbed. I explained what I had done and he told me that he suspected that it only had to do with a battery malfunction for the remote control. He advised that he had cut off the fuel supply of my car as he was not sure that I and the car were safe.

He then said he would reverse the process within two minutes and the car should start. Indeed, I started it after two minutes and he phoned back to check and advised that I should replace the remote unit battery the next morning.

The whole episode left me with a feeling of satisfaction that this firm executed its responsibilities quite efficiently. Second, the concern and courtesy of their employee was extremely comforting. He even assured my wife that there was nothing to worry about when he first phoned her to get my phone number.

Most of our lives we are slaves to tradition and precedent which may well be out of kilter with new circumstances and thus only serve to retard progress. Contemporary corporate history shows that it is those companies which take the risk to break ranks with convention that become success stories. This theme will be demonstrated in the next showcase of the hallmark of service excellence.

THE ART OF PLEASING PEOPLE

The organisation cited as a service excellence benchmark in the ensuing analogy is not of African origin, but has established roots on the continent, buttressed by a cadre of skilled African franchisees and staff. The organisation is McDonald's of the United States of America. From personal experience as one of the first African executives of McDonald's in South Africa, I will take time to narrate the following story.

The USA-based international quick-service restaurant giant established itself in South Africa in 1995 as the entry point into the continent. That was the 84th country on the world map it was occupying, which meant that much replication of its culture and systems. However, South Africa provided a host of challenges such as racial polarisation because of centuries of apartheid; economic and social deprivation of the African people; deeply entrenched cultural traits amongst African ethnic groupings about not eating out; a tradition of labour unrest as a vanguard of political resistance by the masses of the population and an artificially high quality of life among the white population because of the sheltered separate socio-economic system. All these variables do, to some extent, run contrary to the art of service excellence because the playing fields of the population are uneven. These are the odds that the fast-food giant had to brave in setting up shop in South Africa.

The first distinctive feature of the organisation was its devotion to people development, commonly known as staff training. The office opened on 1 April 1995 but of the five senior managers who had signed their employment contracts in the third week of March, three had already begun to work in a country such as Turkey or Australia to start their training. Irrespective of whether one was an accountant, engineer, HR practitioner or anything else one had to undergo intensive training in a McDonald's restaurant somewhere in the world. The training could be a gruelling experience that entailed working long shifts and doing such menial work as cleaning toilets, the floor and tables. All this was designed to acclimatise the new arrival to the mainstay of the organisation, which is QSC & V. This acronym means Quality, Service, Cleanliness and Value for money to the customer. You either love it and stay, or hate it to the same extent and quit early.

Exactly a month after opening the office, some 39 South African young men and women plus three franchisees were sent for six months' training in the Far East, where McDonald's is well established. Three months later another large number followed, and this continued for 18 months. Each group would spend six months training overseas and franchisees took their entire families with them for that period. Not even one restaurant was open before November, which could prompt the simple-minded to question the wisdom of such training expenditure. However, the results of the training were far reaching for both the company and the trainees. Apart from gaining unparalleled world-class expertise in restaurant service, the personalities of the incumbents were permanently enriched by the international exposure. The company was able to transplant completely international McDonald's standards in every respect from those countries to South Africa.

Most of these trainees graduated at the Hamburger University at McDonald's headquarters in Chicago, which is a highly coveted certification in 'hamburgerology' (the art of cooking hamburgers). In practice this meant that by the time the first two restaurants opened in Johannesburg and Cape Town nine months later a highly motivated and skilled group of staff and franchisees operated those restaurants. Just to ensure first-class service all round, some 52 general staff (unskilled) were flown to the same country in the Far East for three weeks' training. It was amazing the attitudinal transformation which occurred in these young people in that short period of time.

One may now ask a myriad of questions such as: How much did this cost? Was it really necessary? Is it sustainable into the future? Is the company reaping the benefits now five years later? Did the trainees benefit? Has all this training benefited the customer?

The answer to the first question is 'millions of rands or dollars' and to the rest it is an unequivocal 'Yes'.

INDOCTRINATION THROUGH TRAINING

It is because of the uniformity and intensity of this training that all McDonald's products look and taste the same in over 100 countries around the world. The BigMac, the chicken, beef and cheese burgers, as well as the famous French fries, are all cooked to a similar temperature in the same manner, on similar equipment and served with a similar smile. Every one of the millions of customers who patronise McDonald's restaurants around the world daily can expect the same fast and friendly service preceded by the same 'Welcome to McDonald's' remark in English, Japanese, French, Italian and any other language.

It was through the power of such training that McDonald's became the world leader in the quick-service restaurant industry. Its focus on customer service goes back to its founder, Ray Kroc, who established such a strong tradition of customer service in 1955. It became the corporate credo that

McDonald's are not in the hamburger business, but in the people service business. The moral lesson here is that customer service excellence is not achieved by accident. It is the result of systematic planning, dedication and hardwork supported by intensive training. Any normal human being is capable of learning the fundamental principles of liking, respecting and meeting customer needs in a fast and friendly way in a congenial environment.

The difference between winning business organisations and losers is primarily lack of staff training. Imagine the number of firms which are managed by people who have never attended one day of managerial training. They in turn employ unskilled people to cut costs and refuse to upgrade them for similar reasons. How many organisations do we come across daily which believe that training is a waste of money, for customers will buy their goods anyway? Indeed such organisations are by far in the majority in Africa. For this reason we are relegated to less than world-class players and we will remain net importers of skills that are supposed to be commonsense. Customer orientation demands a complete overhaul of our approach to business as Africans, to adopt a more sensitive and competitive attitude.

RECIPE FOR SUCCESS THROUGH CUSTOMER CARE

History has proved that success is not an accident. This holds equally true for individuals, organisations, communities and nations. A certain discipline is required of market leaders at every level that involves every component of each respective entity.

The first requirement for service excellence lies in the organisational culture. It must be conducive to excelling in customer care and not inhibiting in any way. Earlier we discussed how the founder of McDonald's built a culture of quality and service excellence that became enshrined in the organisation's, philosophy. The challenge is to perpetuate this culture through the passage of time and technology. It is only possible through a clear and concise vision shared by all employees. Often we see attractively framed vision, mission and values statements in reception areas of organisations. Recently I was very encouraged to see these in the government ministries of Uganda, South Africa and others in Africa. Understanding and commitment to the common vision motivates employees and management towards teamwork as well as supreme achievement. Here is a simple but revealing anecdote. A passerby came across three people working on a project, but they were 20 metres apart. He asked the first person: 'Sir, What are you doing?' The man answered in a dull and sulky tone: 'I am laying bricks.' The passerby proceeded to the next man and asked the same question. The answer was an uninterested but firm: 'I am building a wall.' Then he walked to the third person and asked likewise. This man replied with a smile and lively voice, using gestures pointing out the first two men, and said: 'We are building a cathedral!'

The lesson here is that the third man knew the end result of his effort and the role of his team members. Thus he could already envisage the complete cathedral while his colleagues only saw bricks and mortar. When management share their vision through effective communication and participation they empower the employees to act independently but appropriately.

The second prerequisite for service excellence is positive management and leadership style. While management focuses on efficiency or doing things right here and now, leadership emphasises effectiveness, that is doing the right things at the right time. Thus leadership promotes change in behaviour more than management. Leadership empowers every employee by delegating application of established principles and philosophy of the firm. Another example from McDonald's will help to clarify. The lowest-level employee is trained to minister to customer needs at any time. If a service attendant, commonly termed 'crew person', is unable to give you your order within 45 to 60 seconds he or she must explain it upfront. If a customer complains that the food does not meet the standards of, say, being hot and fresh, the same employee is empowered to correct this to make the customer happy immediately.

It is important to remember that good leadership starts right at the top of the pyramid with the chairman of the board and permeates the hierarchy downwards to the frontline supervisor. This philosophy of management as service leaders and frontline staff as service heroes can be depicted by the concept of the inverted organisation chart below.

CUSTOMERS

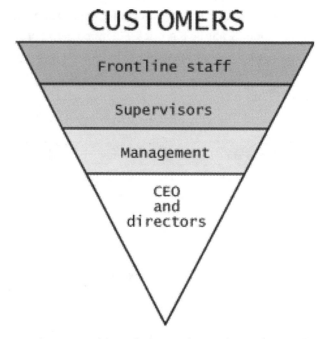

This organogram has several benefits over the traditional one of an upright pyramid. These are:

- *It encourages two-way communication between customers and front-line staff.*
- *Frontliners are empowered to be real service heroes.*
- *The CEO (euphemistically called 'chief empowerment officer') exists to create an enabling environment for all staff to serve the customer well.*

- *It really makes the customer a king in the business.*
- *Top management commitment to service excellence is assured.*

Third, staff are the alpha and omega of service excellence. When willing, they are living advertisements for company products, but when scorned they can be crippling saboteurs. A simple tried-and-tested theory is that satisfied and happy staff will transfer their satisfaction directly to the customer. The same theory applies in reverse to a disgruntled employee. It is more of an uphill battle to win a single new customer than to retain existing ones. However, for a company to keep abreast of inflationary trends in Africa, it must increase its sales by at least 20% per annum. No wonder that the mortality rate of organisations is considerable in this part of the world.

High employee productivity and commitment to customers begins with sowing the right seed. This means if you recruit people with either the right skills or the potential for a good fit you are well onto the winning formula. Then follows training targeted at developing specific skills, which must have the ultimate effect of enhancing service. Skills development is the best insurance for organisational success and against bankruptcy. In Africa training also carries a special extra component of bridging the cultural gap between eurocentric and afrocentric business approaches. The two are not mutually exclusive and realistic training should close the gapm by creating greater understanding of either side. The most critical training is that which inculcates basic skills of the trade, followed by broader social and behavioural skills at higher levels.

The concept of internal and external customers should be discussed at this juncture. Every organisation serves two types of customer, namely internal and external. The former are all employees of the firm in so far as they relate to one another. Each department must view other departments and employees as its customers and treat them as such. More so, management must view their subordinates as their customers whose needs must be taken seriously.

'External customers' refers to the public who buy services and products from the organisation. In common parlance this is the only category viewed as customers. This is an erroneous myopic view of the dynamic nature of customer service. Market leaders insist that: 'Every position in an organisation must serve the external customer directly, or an internal customer who in turn serves the external one. If it does neither, it must be eliminated because it is superfluous.'

Close on the heels of optimal staffing is the phenomenon of reward and punishment. There is abundant evidence in various theories of motivation that human beings respond to stimuli in the appropriate context. Reward comes in many forms, including indirect reward such as public compliment, personal recognition, and direct reward in cash. The corollary is to punish behaviour that negates service excellence. The punishment must be directly linked to the failure both in terms of timing and relevance.

The next principle is to live up to the moments of truth. Each frontline employee in contact with a customer represents both his or her organisation and his or her supervisors. Each time that one gets in contact directly or otherwise with a customer that is a moment of truth. You have only 30 seconds to impress the customer, which will last a long time. Key behaviours to help meet this challenge include dispensing only high-quality service and products. It also woos customers when they see evidence of commitment to and passion for the product being offered. Indeed all this is possible through dedicated hard work at every stage. It should be remembered that the road to quality service is long and has no end. Accordingly, it is painfully true that laziness and apathy never yield customer satisfaction.

The last principle is commitment to stopping the rot on the African continent. Every economically active person should be mindful of the existence and demands of the global village. Advancements in technology and management science bring the five continents together daily. Increasingly, we witness major transcontinental investments such as large USA companies re-investing in South Africa and leading South African firms listing on the New York, London, and other major world stock exchanges.

The net result is that competition intensifies, performance demands are heightened, and the sole competitive edge becomes the finite attention to customer needs. This necessitates a real commitment to African and ultimately global enhancement. There is no doubt that a private sector of any size has the responsibility and wherewithal to create and uphold the dream of the African renewal.

THE TOTAL APPROACH

If one is seeking a service revolution, where does one start? Success will require an integrated, sustained and total approach. Our discussion of masters of service excellence endeavoured to reveal the critical success factors. To complement this winning formula, let us conclude with five key managerial actions which lead to a comprehensive service package.

TOP MANAGEMENT COMMITMENT

Success through service is neither accidental nor a fluke of fortunate happenstances. It has to be well planned to include all the resources within and at the disposal of the organisation. Customer service initiatives are much more than training events. They are a well-coordinated process rather than a stop-start series of events provoked by temporary need.

Training is one component in a total organisational approach to the pursuit of service excellence. Employees taking part in that training are greatly motivated by seeing that 'top people' are fully committed to the initiative and it is much more than 'flavour of the month' fallacy. The service philosophy must be marketed internally with great emphasis before attempting to transform the external customers. To this end it is crucial to have all managers committed to a service initiative. The values underlying the programme need to be defined, communicated and modelled by the top team. This will often involve changes in the organisational structure to provide the frontliners with much greater authority to make decisions

49

involving the customer. Such empowerment not only motivates the employee but it gives the customer a feeling of being valued by a responsible organisation.

Nothing infuriates a customer so much as being referred through a chain of people to get a problem solved. The first person should be ready and able to solve it, for this is the moment of truth when the customer meets the human face of the organisation.

Unless all the managers are committed, this can appear a threat to their authority, causing them to undermine the effort. Line managers should be key players whose task is to lead, market and model the service programme. If they are not given this role, they most likely become progress blockers and saboteurs. In the extreme of top management commitment to the 'McDonald's way' of customer service, Ray Kroc, the founder of the organisation, would personally pick up paper in the parking lot of a McDonald's restaurant. Every person goes through a five-step training course, which was developed and standardised within the world-wide corporation to instill skills of serving customers from general worker to restaurant manager. That transforms the system from selling hamburgers to dispensing customer service.

COMPANY VISION OWNERSHIP

Service training must be seen as flowing from the firm's vision or mission. Knowing where the firm sees its future, knowing its aspirations, its values, ambitions and targets allows staff to see the purpose of and rationale for a quality service initiative. Vision is that intangible and cognitive future state of affairs which motivates employees to action. It gives the direction where you are going and should be like a mirage – within sight but just out of reach. The major purposes of a company vision in relation to customer service are:

- *It shows visible evidence of the company's priorities and commitment.*
- *It lights the flame to spur staff to action.*

- *It serves as the clarion call which gathers the troops and concentrates on the task at hand.*
- *It represents the destination of the journey to the promised land.*
- *It sets the benchmark for judging the company.*
- *It inspires and provokes the corporate mind.*

Thus vision is the rallying cry which mobilises people and supplies impetus to make them believe that 'we can do it', and they will.

Let us bring the concept closer to reality by recalling some of the famous visions of this century. In 1960 President of the USA, John F Kennedy, envisioned that 'We will put a man on the moon within a decade'. This inspired the whole nation and mobilised enormous funds to fulfil that vision, which in fact occurred before the deadline.

In 1964, Martin Luther King Jnr inspired the civil rights movement in USA with his vision of 'I have a dream ... That one day all races shall live together in harmony'. His dream shaped the minds of Americans towards human rights and continues to do so as well as influencing many nations around the globe.

Again in 1964, at the Rivonia Trial, Nelson Mandela, later to become the first black president of South Africa, cast a vision which has influenced the history of the country ever since. Faced with the real possibility of a death sentence for alleged treason he said: 'All my lifetime I have devoted myself to the struggle of the African People ... I have cherished the ideal of a free and democratic society ... It is an ideal which I hope to live for and achieve. Also, for which I am prepared to die' (Mandela 1900). This vision mobilised public opinion at home and abroad, and kept the freedom torch alight for nearly three decades while he was incarcerated in prison. It kept him and national hope alive awaiting the promised land.

These are the practical benefits of a vision in a family, community, company or nation. Companies with clear visions incorporating customer care have a distinctly better chance of achieving service excellence than those which fly by the seats of their pants.

CUSTOMER SERVICE RESEARCH

According to Jan Carlzon (1987), the legendary turnaround chief executive of Scandanavian Airline Systems, it has been proved that when employees are well trained in customer service they develop heightened sensitivity about customers. They can easily and confidently answer these crucial questions. 'Who are our customers? What do they want or expect from me?' These questions are fundamental to the pursuit of service excellence. The most successful organisations are in constant dialogue with their customers, in an effort to learn about their needs and interests. Success can only come from regular provision of what customers want, in the form they want it, at the time and place where they want it. This requires keeping in touch with customer opinions. There are several such customer outreach programmes. First and foremost they start with employee satisfaction evaluation. A simple employee opinion survey regarding service circumstances, reward levels, work conditions and relationships in service situations always yields useful information.

The next step is to undertake periodic customer satisfaction surveys at least once per annum but preferably more regularly. Some surveys are done on each moment of truth by asking a customer to complete a service questionnaire at the conclusion of the service transaction. Most hotels ask guests to complete a questionnaire when checking out. However, such cases of genuine customer care are few and far between.

ALL-ENCOMPASSING TRAINING

Successful businesses identify employees as internal customers and the public as external customers. This concept seeks to promote the attitudes and skills which underpin excellence in customer service. It needs also to establish that the quality of service to external customers begins with the quality of service that people or departments provide to one another in-house. How can a department treat external customers well if it ill-treats its own workers? The answer is that it is most probable that it will extend the same rough treatment to outsiders, causing them not to come back again. This observation goes a long way towards ensuring that the quality of service associated with an organisation is only as good as the internal customer service rendered to one another by its employees. The most pertinent training adds practical skills of handling customers and meeting their needs. It starts with a certain level of functional literacy to enable the incumbent to read and write basic communication standards. Then follows systematic simple modular training which relates to the practical work undertaken by the person. Team exercises consolidate learned skills more effectively than individual effort. There should be standard methods of evaluating the success of the training, leading to identifiable rewards to reinforce the learning.

Most of all, skills training can only flourish in an environment conducive to the use of the learned skills. For this to happen, management must have undergone similar and more advanced training. Their behaviour should change to supporting what is advocated by the training. All training must have one single objective, that of enhancing customer service. To this end managers and frontliners must learn from their mistakes as well as complaints of bad service. That is the essence of a learning organisation which continually keeps ahead of the rate of change.

FOLLOW-THROUGH PROCESS

The act of generating the energy and skills which will promote customer service excellence produces a need to harness, manage and channel what the training produces. A key feature of any initiative needs to be the strategies and systems for ensuring follow-through. Unless the products of the training can be applied, rewarded, reviewed and monitored, then its full potential may not be realised. This activity rests on the axiom which says 'trust but verify' every action to check negative impact. (The next section seeks to attune our minds to the crucial role of internationalisation of our continent to access the skills and economic means to enhance customer service in different situations.)

AFRICAN GLOBALISATION AND SERVICE EXCELLENCE

Multinational or transnational corporations are the most prevalent method of foreign direct investment and propagation of business practices. It is not coincidence that the dominant corporations in Africa originate from the former colonial powers of Europe such as Britain, Germany, Portugal, Spain and Italy. USA and Canada are new arrivals and together with Japan have become the biggest origin of multinational businesses because of their economic domination of the world. But is the spread of foreign business around the world as bad as political colonisation? Is it another form of colonisation? What benefits, if any, accrue to the host country of the multinational business?

First, foreign investment through the establishment of business subsidiaries by TNCs (transnational corporations) is an integral part of globalisation which cannot be stopped. It should not be perceived in the same way as political domination because it is fundamentally driven by a process completely separate from the political machinery of its home country. In most Western countries, business is completely different from politics and therefore free to chart its own destiny and relationships around the world. Of course a business firm will not wantonly disregard the foreign policy of its home government and invest in a country politically hostile to its own nation. I urge my fellow Africans to view foreign investment as an apolitical relationship and not a reincarnation of colonisation.

Having said that, I believe that transnational corporations should invest through partnerships with local businesses and individuals of the host country. Good examples are oil companies which operate through a network of local distributors, Coca-Cola and McDonald's, which empower local franchisees and transfer ownership to them through business partnership. Indeed 100 per cent ownership of the business enterprise by a foreign corporation smacks of total dominance and exploitative intentions.

Third, if foreign investment is handled well and honestly, several benefits accrue to both parties. The host country stands to gain in the long term in a number of ways. In the first instance, the employment creation capacity of TNCs offers much-needed jobs to local citizens, and in most cases specific skills development programmes are mounted to induct the new entrants into the new business culture. In some cases (such as McDonald's) the training is so elaborate and structured that it is linked directly to the career progression of an individual from the lowest level to restaurant manager and beyond. The fact that such high potential staff are sent to the Hamburger University in Chicago means their mental horizons are broadened with a new international service standard yardstick. Coca-Cola similarly upgrades its operations through training at its headquarters in Atlanta and so do many other TNCs such as IBM, Shell, BP, Standard Chartered Bank, Barclays Bank, Microsoft and Toyota.

In addition to exposing local business to international service standards, TNCs also help to expose it to the international fray of corporate governance scrutiny. This inevitably improves professionalism in corporate management, which leads to organisational stability. Although remote, the existence of TNCs adds to the economic stability of a country as they create wealth, which boosts the local gross domestic product. Higher GDP results in higher per capita income which, all being equal, assists in creating political stability.

Therefore, while TNCs benefit from the profits reaped in return for their investment and they find sanctuary for some of their personnel who may not have a place in their home country; they play a constructive role in the process of internationalising Africa. Thus TNCs are real players in the quest for service excellence.

Chapter 3

The customer service concept in the political arena

What is the common thread that cuts across all the continents regarding politics? Cast your mind around the world and think of some past and present heads of state: Ronald Reagan of USA, Queen Elizabeth II of Britain, Fidel Castro of Cuba, Helmut Kohl of Germany, Kim Il Sung of North Korea, Boris Yeltsin of Russia, Kamuzu Banda of Malawi, Kenneth Kaunda of Zambia, Robert Mugabe of Zimbabwe, Daniel Arap Moi of Kenya, Sam Nujoma of Namibia, Milton Obote of Uganda and King Sobhuza II of Swaziland. Look at their age profile and tenure of office. It is amazing that of all highly paid employment, politics is the only occupation where there is no formal contract of employment which enforces retirement at the conventional age of 60 or 65. I have respectfully omitted Nelson Mandela of South Africa, Quett Masire of Botswana and Julius Nyerere of Tanzania as elder statesmen of Africa. Each had the wisdom to know when to exit active politics, although it was for different reasons. In other words, they were sufficiently sensitive to the needs of their followers as their customers to know when they had ceased to satisfy them.

Nelson Mandela had to take up the presidency of the new South Africa at the age of 75 because of his incarceration by previous Afrikaner regimes. However, he made it clear at the outset that he was racing against time and would retire after one term of office. Anyone who is familiar with the humility of this wonderful man would probably conclude that he would not have particularly wanted to become president any way, but was compelled by love for his country and people to conclude his life struggle by establishing the foundation for justice, equality, human dignity, prosperity and peace in South Africa. I have met many African heads of state and am familiar with the aura of demi-godness that they create around them.

Nelson Mandela is the opposite of this as a national leader and this sets contrasting lessons in customer orientation in politics.

Is it not a contradiction in philosophy in the same society that the convention seems to be that a chief executive of a large corporation is expected to retire at 60 years because he is tired, but a politician is allowed to run a whole country and influence world affairs when he or she is well past retirement age? Are these double standards a deliberate oversight by the various societies? It also appears that a tendency to stay too long at the helm prevails in the poorer nations of the world, which brings the spotlight onto Africa. Why does this phenomenon prevail? Is it not lack of customer orientation on the part of political leaders?

PRESIDING OVER SUBJECTS OR FOLLOWERS?

To place this discussion into its correct perspective, let us exclude the monarchy system of leadership such as is practised in the United Kingdom, Swaziland and Lesotho. In these systems the term 'subjects' may still be acceptable although contemporary politics in Swaziland and Lesotho are now challenging that subservient status of the populace. In the non-monarchy system of government do the political leaders see the population as their subjects or followers? The answer is predominantly the former, much to our amazement. If it were the opposite, politicians would not see themselves as being above the constituent electorate which voted them into power to the extent of becoming dictators and squashing any criticism while causing economic and social degradation.

There are several examples on our continent such as that involving the president of Namibia, Sam Nujoma. When the country gained its political independence, a constitution was written providing for a maximum of two presidential terms of office. It was hailed as the most progressive national constitution in a continent of lifelong rulers. However, when Nujoma's second term of office was coming to an end, he started manoeuvres to have the constitution amended to scrap the limiting clause. The grounds adduced by his cronies for such abrogation of constitutional integrity were that 'he was the only leader of such ability and distinction that he is loved and respected by all people'. Is this not a ridiculous overassertion in a society of millions of people of different talents? Obviously, the explanation lies in the fact that 'power corrupts and absolute power corrupts absolutely'. He started off as a good selfless revolutionary leader who is now turning into a dictator because he has tested unbridled power and liked it. The revolution has lost its way and the masses who were his comrades and elevated him to power are now 'subjects' who can no longer influence his behaviour. This holier-than-thou illusion pervades the entire African continent except in a few isolated cases. Because of such stark realities one can confidently conclude that in the main African politicians do not view their electorate as their customers but as a means to an end, that being their ascension to power. This goes against the grain of the customer orientation philosophy discussed in earlier chapters. The above story comes as no surprise to those who know the historical friendship between Sam Nujoma and Robert Mugabe, who has been president of Zimbabwe since 1980. Birds of a feather flock together, so the wise profess.

THE ZIMBABWE BOOMERANG EFFECT

Since the tumultuous developments of early 2000 in Zimbabwe are current at the time of writing, they warrant close scrutiny against the philosophy of service excellence. The brief background is that the Zanu PF Party, under Robert Mugabe, has been ruling the country since April 1980, when the minority Rhodesia Front under Ian Smith lost power in a watershed majority parliamentary election. Like every nation that gained its independence from colonial rule, Zimbabweans celebrated the dawn of a new era of democracy, economic prosperity, international citizenship and higher quality of life in every respect. The first five years were quite close to this dream, but thereafter the gulf between reality and the promised land became increasingly visible. A spirit of societal despair prevailed until early 1999 when a working-class-driven political party emerged as the Movement for Democratic Change. Nine months later it contested the general election in June 2000 and won 48% of the parliamentary seats. This was an unprecedented show of dissension from the 'liberation ideology' of not breaking ranks. Why did these millions of people suddenly change their loyalty base? It was simply because they had watched their quality of life deteriorate rapidly because of the political supremacy of the Zanu PF leadership which relegated them to the level of puppets with no say in their own destiny. Society was no longer receiving the service it deserved from politicians and public servants. Corruption and nepotism took over from pragmatic public policy dispensation.

The first act of supplanting customer service by Mugabe and Zanu PF was to create an environment of a de facto one-party state to dictate the political process. This robbed the citizenry of the freedom of choice and created similar monopolistic malaise to lack of competition in the business market. The second act of service sabotage was the manipulation of the constitution by a handful of political bigots, which gave credence to a political hegemony in which loyalty and not competence were rewarded. Naturally this isolated the masses who were not connected to the hierarchy. Again, such practice flies in the face of any principle of customer service, particularly the age-old 'the customer is king'. The third flagrant breach of service excellence principles by Robert Mugabe and Zanu PF was to regiment society and try to resuscitate the pre-1980 racial division as emotional blackmail to win the election. This gave rise to the violence and total breakdown of the rule of law that entailed private farm invasions and deaths of innocent people.

All these sentiments were aptly expressed by the *Financial Gazette* of Zimbabwe on 29 June 2000. Under the bold heading 'A travesty of justice' the paper said:

> That Zimbabwe's just-ended watershed general election would be a farce
> was predictable. Predictable because conditions for a free and fair ballot

never existed and because the governing Zanu PF party would not allow democracy to triumph in a country it holds up as its fiefdom ... Just when the nation had united in a rare show of force to bring about powerful change and end the people's suffering of two decades, the ruling party responded by brutalising them in the futile hope of postponing the inevitable – its demise ... Again this was ignored in a mirror of high-handedness and arrogance that have come to symbolise the only enduring legacy of this government. For all the outward calm that pervades Zimbabwe, there is seething anger in the population that the country, once a beacon of hope in blighted Africa, has been allowed to crumble this way.

This is a powerful summary of how citizens can enforce their right to good service as customers to the leadership. They could not get the desired level of service and joined hands across racial and ethnic lines to vote for change – not necessarily a political dogma – but change that serves their interests as well as those of posterity. This has to be a classic case study in the modern African political history of change.

AFRICAN TRADITION VS POLITICS OF DEMOCRACY

Let us examine the causality and possible cultural origin of these dictatorial tendencies. Historically the tribal chief was an unchallenged benevolent dictator whose power base was ascribed by tradition. His every behaviour was regulated by societal norms and the value system which he observed religiously. There was an inherent sense of morality, transparency and benevolence in the leader which pre-empted any exploitative tendencies. It was accepted that the chief was above his subjects but never out of reach and what he had he shared with them in times of need. Owing to these virtues there were no political coups in African society and leaders were dedicated to serving their subjects as their customers. There was relative equality within the social ranking in the society. The only wars were either inter-tribal skirmishes or family feuds over inheritance, which were few and far between. This calmness and serenity seems gone for ever. Perhaps present-day leaders have become highly individualistic at the expense of serving their customers. Why?

POWER VS SERVICE

The answer lies in the phenomenon of the politics of scarcity. Africa was the last continent to develop in terms of modern standards, which resulted in a limitation of resources to satisfy its burgeoning population. Consequently politicians take advantage of their positions of leadership to enrich themselves. This is borne out by the proliferation of prosecutions of political leaders for embezzlement of funds or misappropriation of public property in their charge.

I remember a politician in Zimbabwe who successfully campaigned for a parliamentary seat by handing out blankets to the poor rural constituency. Unbeknown to the grateful recipients, the blankets were a consignment donated by Western Europeans to the poor which he had intercepted using his political standing. The community were so gullible, being a product of the African tradition of not challenging a leader but entrusting him with their own wellbeing instead. Unscrupulous politicians deliberately take advantage of the traditional belief of their electorate in the precept of one tribe, one chief.

Many of us witness every day the disturbing spectacle of 20-vehicle and motorcycle entourages, including bullet-proof armoured vehicles, escorting our political leaders. The already jam-packed city streets are virtually closed to the public at peak periods for one person to go to a political rally. What breeds this godlike feeling of supremacy? One can be sure that it is not because of respect or concern for the populace, but brazen arrogance. Why is it that in all African societies, although almost all of them are plagued with poverty and protracted revolutionary fighting, politicians and their close kindred always live in comparative luxury? The answer is simply that, unlike the chiefs of yesteryear who were selfless and kept close to their folk, today's leaders are obsessed with power and social distinction. As a result, coup d'etats are the order of the day as disaffected citizens feel compelled to change the order, but find that all possible avenues of normal change are deliberately blocked.

In Zimbabwe a bitter war was waged for decades against the foreign colonial power. By virtue of historical rural upbringing, the closest thing to the heart of an African is land. Likewise, the political leaders fired up the revolution by promising the return of the land to the destitute masses. In response, schoolchildren and adults went to war and won after more than a decade. Every one of them expected the payback to materialise soon after peace returned with political change. Instead, the senior politicians grabbed repossessed land for themselves. The landless masses were left out in the cold as the political elite parcelled out large tracts of land for themselves and their followers. The few hundreds of peasants who were resettled were not equipped with basic intensive farming skills, which resulted in poor productivity and sporadic famine in a country of historically abundant food supplies. This has enlarged the gap between the haves and the have-nots, leading to major tensions across the entire society. The national constitution has also been amended many times in the 20 years of independence to entrench dictatorial tendencies in the political leadership.

We are continually bombarded with news of unethical conduct by political leaders of all colours and races in our region. In South Africa a prominent member of the ruling party bought thousands of party membership cards to inflate her list of voter support at the national conference. In the same vein, another local leader of the official opposition Democratic party was also involved in scandal for inflating party membership with people who were deceased, had resigned or had moved. This was a white party official of a predominantly white political party, which shows that public impropriety is not limited to blacks.

In Zambia, just before their last presidential elections at the turn of the twentieth century, the president tried to steamroller legislation through the judiciary and parliamentary system to declare former president Kenneth Kaunda a non-citizen. This was a blatant attempt to nullify Kaunda's candidacy as a challenger for the presidential seat. Such revelations of poor transparency and accountability unfortunately tarnish the image of the African political scenario.

. However, there is a silver lining in the seemingly sad cloud of bad governance. Success stories in some African countries counter the image of coups in Nigeria, Sierra Leone, Ivory Coast and the Democratic Republic of Congo as well as dictatorship and genocide in Ethiopia, Sudan, Rwanda and Angola, among others.

The events of smooth political leadership which occurred in South Africa, Botswana, Tanzania and many decades ago in Gambia are worthy of the utmost African pride. Nelson Mandela began to groom Thabo Mbeki as his successor within a year of becoming the first president of a democratic South Africa. The handover was so smooth that it perpetuated social stability, economic growth and international confidence in the country. A year earlier Sir Ketumile Masire had handed over the presidency of Botswana to Festus Mogae under a similar planned succession. The example had been set by the late Julius Nyerere in the mid-1980s when he relinquished the presidency of Tanzania to Hasan Mwinyi. What do these three African statesmen have in common?

They were all invited by other nations and international bodies to be facilitators in conflict resolution and economic development. The late Nyerere was the founder chair of the South-South Commission and mediator in the Burundi conflict in equatorial Africa. After Nyerere's death in 1999 Nelson Mandela was invited to take up the role. He had already played an active role between Israel and Palestine and had the distinction of breaking the log-jam between Libya and the United Nations over the Lockerbie bombing in Scotland. Ketumile Masire has also been invited by the various rebel groups to act as peace broker in the Democratic Republic of Congo. These three leaders displayed service excellence in their countries by selflessly delivering better quality of life to the rank and file. They lived up to the true humility and honesty of the traditional African leader of the past.

WHAT THE HUMBLE CUSTOMERS EXPECT

One of the fundamental principles of customer service excellence is a display of inherent respect for the customer. This leads to honest and dignified treatment of any individual or group with the potential of being a customer to yourself. After all, money in the cash register shows no colour, gender or racial distinction. It is still the cherished dream of millions of Africans across the continent that one day they will have politicians who will treat them like customers in every respect. These are the customers who eagerly and humbly expect service excellence from their political leaders. Imagine how refreshing it would be to have a national leader who genuinely and publicly announces that: 'I am answerable to the people of this country, and I am not above them. I will serve them first before myself and my relatives.'

A utopian world of service excellence would provide a society which offers a similar starting point in life for all citizens; a concerned cadre of selfless politicians and national leaders who promote community progress; leaders who respect the people and tell them the truth at all times to enable appropriate decision making; and leaders who do not erect artificial social barriers in front of their electorate in order to live in a world of plenty amidst abject poverty. Thus, even politicians must live by the key behaviours of customer service.

The typical African is amenable to authority by virtue of traditional socialisation. He does not wantonly challenge leadership, but instead tends to accept authority unquestioningly. In contrast, most leaders do not reciprocate the trust and respect placed on them, but exploit them as a weakness in their customers.

A MODEL POLITICAL SERVICE LEADER

Political leadership is very much a thankless job, as one cannot satisfy the diverse needs of all people all the time. The concept of the majority is the guiding principle, which gives some comfort of mind. Political leadership also brings risk to the incumbent and sometimes his or her families. This is borne out by many cases of assassinations, either by rivals from outside or rebel elements from within the same fraternity. The paradox is that in monetary terms a political career is not the most rewarding in any society. Even the American dream of unlimited opportunities could not make the president's remuneration equal to that of the chief executive officer or chairman of a private sector corporation. This anomaly is even more glaring in the relatively poor nations of Africa, where the economies simply cannot afford inflated compensation packages.

So why do people go to great lengths to run for political office against the backdrop of such restricted rewards? No wonder that one never sees a queue of bright young professionals applying for political jobs, for they have more attractive avenues to exploit. However, the motivation to enter the political arena is manifold. Reasons include genuine commitment to serving the community, a desire to change the status quo positively; the lack of lucrative economic opportunities elsewhere; an abundance of entry-level possibilities; and a deep-seated need for power. Consequently, it becomes a self-fulfilling prophecy that because the top brains of society shun politics, the less committed fill the political positions almost by default. This leads to wide-spread substandard service to powerless customers. One has yet to devise a formula for attracting and nurturing young talent in the political field which would eventually upgrade the level of professionalism and service leadership in the African context.

Although the primary focus of this book is the organisational context, the broader national and international playground of leadership impacts continuously on the performance of the former. Politicians provide a broader context in which organisations must conduct their task. The economy, international trading and taxation laws, social change, violence and the quality of education all impact on the ability of organisations to compete internationally.

Consequently the quality of political leadership is a vital ingredient of national growth. In a research exercise in 1993, *Time* magazine established that an enormous gap existed between supply of and demand for political leadership, which created bigger and more pervasive problems than ineffectual organisational leadership. It was concluded the vast majority of world leaders have been ill prepared for their roles and have not been trained for leading in a new world with new changes. Under such circumstances of dearth of skills it is not surprising that the world is aflame with wars, internal civil strife within nations and ethnic purges. Africa has claimed its place in the centrestage of these gross human rights violations.

WHAT IS LEADERSHIP?

The acid test of effective leadership is not what you do but the way that you do it. First, leadership is defined in the eyes of the followers and not the leader's own perception. Second, effective leadership entails empowering the followers to develop into leaders in their own right. It is in this aspect of promoting a self-sustaining growth capacity in followers that most African political leaders fall down.

THE VIRTUES OF SERVANT LEADERSHIP

Political constituents like to see their leaders personally and no substitute will do. In addition to visibility, political leaders should be guided by an even tighter set of ethics than a business manager. The following profile of a political leader should suffice as a guide:

First, there is a need for professional tenets to guide the leader's behaviour in his or her dealings with the electorate. Servant leadership hails from the philosophy that in order to lead, one must first serve. Listening to people, serving real needs, empowering the populace, developing communities, thinking globally, acting ethically and affirming individual dignity and worth, these are the hallmarks of political leadership in the twenty-first century.

Second, a political leader must be an accomplished manager of people and problem-solving processes. Leadership is the essential ingredient in successful human endeavour at every level of local, national and international life. Unless leaders equip themselves adequately for their role, they are not only shooting themselves in the foot, but also their organisations in the heart.

Third is the internally generated achievement need. A leader must predominantly be achievement driven and tireless in order to cultivate sustainable energy to pursue sometimes elusive goals. Complementary characteristics are internal satisfaction and emotional equilibrium. An undue level of desperation induces a leader to vacillate between the ends of the psychological pendulum, resulting in erratic decision making. Furthermore, a leader must be sufficiently thick-skinned to absorb propaganda effects and public criticism even where it is not warranted.

Fourth is the phenomenon of leaders' accountability to their constituents. They must always be cognisant of the mandate given by their electorate and should never overstep it by devious means. In the same vein is the crucial quality of transparency of leadership processes and actions. Leaders also need to be held accountable for developing and communicating a clear and concise goal for the future. Simultaneously, the leader must take cognisance of the reality of restraining forces, which inhibit the realisation of that cardinal goal.

Fifth is the concept of leadership courage. Leaders need to have the courage to see the existing situation as it really is and to encourage feedback on the progress of their strategies and the personal impact on their followers. In this respect bad news is better than no news. This means that leaders should consciously encourage devil's advocates who have an honest but different view. The temptation of many leaders is to surround themselves with sycophants who always tell the leader what he wants to hear. This is a common trait in African society where it is aggravated by the cultural indoctrination that the leader is incorruptable, all-knowing and omnipotent. Appraisal of the leader's performance is interpreted as undermining his authority. Therefore, there is ample merit in consultative and participative leadership.

Sixth comes the need to be 'with the people' at the coalface. This is the most effective way of picking up problems and communicating the leadership vision. The paradox is that most leaders do not want to get their hands dirty but they expect to win. Leaders simply commit professional suicide if they are not visible and accessible. This is more than simply boasting that 'I have an open door policy', which in most cases people are too scared to use. A model leader is a genuine people-lover, an integrationist and a reconciler of diverse views. Too many political leaders in Africa unashamedly use divisive tactics to promote political faction-alism, which often results in bloodshed and anarchy.

In seventh place is the folly of leaders' self-defeating paradigms of the world and people in general. These are often manifested in negative attitudes and stereotypes towards people such as women and those subjected to historical discrimination. Very often these worldviews are not tested or analysed. As a result, the majority of political parties in Africa are based on ethnic, tribal racial or colour classification. This is a recipe for failure from the outset.

Eighth is a call on leaders to take a stand and be consistent in their actions. Organisational trust is not necessarily generated by telling people what they want to hear, but by consistency and congruence in word and deed, including an unequivocal statement of action and intent that people learn to rely on. Until leaders, whether in the political or business arena, are willing to pay the price for change themselves, they cannot expect others to do so. Once again let us remember the virtues of servant leadership that accrue to those leaders who are constantly learning and thus always outpace the speed of change around them.

SALVATION THROUGH THE AFRICAN RENAISSANCE

It is not all doom and gloom. The much-talked about African Renaissance is not merely political claptrap, but a real paradigm shift. The philosophy dates back to the early 1960s when statesmen such as Kwame Nkrumah of Ghana preached pan-Africanism; Julius Nyerere of Tanzania advocated the spirit of Ujamaa to symbolise togetherness; Jomo Kenyatta of Kenya orchestrated Uhuru to symbolise freedom across the nations and Kenneth Kaunda of Zambia waved his symbolic white handkerchief, spreading the culture of humanism, manifesting mutual helpfulness and respect.

Some of these leaders and their successors have made great efforts to uphold service-oriented governance in their countries. Several introduced leadership or moral codes to guide the public conduct of political and public leaders. The rationale was to encourage leaders to observe the rule of law and lead by example in their interaction with the public. Whilst these initiatives were laudable, they were mostly defeated by the mentality of entitlement which pushes leaders to grab money-making opportunities before lesser people can get them.

However, a silver lining is still manifested in many service-oriented activities aimed at upgrading the quality of life of the citizens. Although these are mostly motivated by a mentality of villagism and tribalism among politicians, the end result can be perceived as good service by expectant customers. Here are a few enlightening historical observations.

Most African societies have been mobilised into mass political parties which seek to devolve power to the grass roots. This followed revolutionary success over colonial political systems, which tipped the power balance from elitist to mass politics. In a sense this has bridged the chasm between traditional communalism and the present parliamentary dispensation. It has heightened a sense of worth and access to service in the mind of the common person. Those countries that have been able to grow genuine mass leadership are reaping the rewards through societal satisfaction and peace. Uganda in Equatorial East Africa is highly symbolic of this successful transformation from one of the worst dictatorships on this continent.

The mentality of villagism creates a parochial approach to service on the part of politicians. To this end it is commonplace to see social and infrastructural development projects taking place firstly and mostly in the home areas of influential political leaders. This includes the construction of roads, dams, irrigation schemes, schools and hospitals. While this could be seen as irregular behaviour by the leaders, the end justifies the means. They marshal much-needed resources for their own home areas, although neglecting those constituencies not strongly represented.

Some national constitutions provide for the office of an ombudsman or public protector. This is a clear attempt to enable the electorate to seek redress for wrongdoing by public officers. In the main, these arbitrators are accountable only to Parliament to enable them to service the entire society unfettered.

Another gesture of political customer service borrows from the caring nature of the traditional chief. Africa is increasingly susceptible to climatic upheavals, which cause famine because of drought or floods. In response to these national disasters some political leaders have come to the aid of the needy by organising handouts of food, seed and agricultural inputs for the following season. In a distant fashion one can say this is a modernisation of the role played by the chief in the past to protect his subjects from any mishap.

However, there are interesting paradoxes that emanate from this political approach and impact negatively on ultimate service excellence by politicians. The election system is foreign to Afrocentric cultures because it implicitly forces people to make a negative choice against their own kin. An African is inherently a consensus-driven individual. Elections tend to create internal psychological dissonance as they sometimes imply breaking ranks with family and friends. Some unscrupulous politicians take advantage of this cultural trait by exacerbating individual uncertainty. Here are some illustrations of recent occurrences.

In the 1950s and 1960s the continent was on fire through civil uprisings to overthrow colonial regimes. The Mau Mau uprising in Kenya and resistance marches in South Africa, Zimbabwe, Malawi, Zambia, Mozambique and many other countries were all motivated by the fight against a common enemy. When this enemy was removed, political rivalry became violent, leading to factional killings among the rank and file as well as the leaders. This was caused by a culture of intolerance of dissension. Political differences were exploited by leaders as the cause of enmity. It was often most successfully based on tribal lines as an African needs no persuasion that one tribe must have only one chief.

The other intriguing political manifestation is the rejection of election results by the general electorate or political leaders. A plethora of reasons can be given, including not being free and fair, intimidation and rigging of votes. Often this forms the bedrock of civil uprisings or even a coup d'etat by revolutionary soldiers or civilians. If one looks at the fundamental causes, one finds that customer service has been short-circuited by the political leaders. They have wedged political intolerance among the masses by denying them the right to decide whether the product or results meet their needs or not. Furthermore, the electorate have been presented with a fait accompli and not a choice. The end result is that customer service has been compromised blatantly, with decision making being removed from the grass roots. The new wave of democracy seeks to reinforce among politicians this sensitivity to serving the ultimate customer.

But one can rightly conclude that the fundamentals for service excellence in the African context exist in the culture. For example, the noble phenomenon of political reconciliation between former white oppressors and the indigenous black populations is an African creation. This has been implemented by political leaders in Zimbabwe, Mozambique,

Namibia, South Africa, Uganda and many others with notable success. Sometimes these gestures of nationhood have been misconstrued as a weakness of the African who has conceded all to the former oppressor without the whites giving up much in return. This is an endless debate but what is more important is that the unique capacity for forgiveness inherent in the African people which makes reconciliation possible. Thus, it is possible for African politicians to deliver customer satisfaction.

SERVICE EXCELLENCE THROUGH POLITICAL DEMOCRACY

Switzerland is indisputably one of the most politically stable, economically advanced and progressive countries of the world. It is also the least politically regimented society of our time with no prominent government and head of state. As a nation, it is merely a constellation of cantons or localities which operate in unison and harmony under democratic governance. The population enjoy an acclaimed high standard of living. Historically the world admired its political neutrality sufficiently to vote it the safest place to store financial and gold surplusses, including some of the spoils of the Nazi German war. It can therefore be safely concluded that political democracy creates an enabling environment in which service delivery to the citizens at political level, customers at business level and member states at international level becomes possible to its optimum.

Chapter 4

Service orientation in the public service sector

In this context the public service sector covers the broad activity field embracing government departments, municipalities, local government authorities and quasi-government business enterprises. The political and legislative arm of government has been discussed extensively already, which restricts this discussion to the executive function of government including related bodies influenced by it. This is the sphere which has the most influence on the economic, social and political lives of people in all African countries since public service and parastatals are by far the biggest formal employers. This makes them the fulcrum around which societal values, work ethic and quality of life perception revolve.

CHRONICLE OF SERVICE HIJACK EVENTS

To bring the point home here are real-life cases, some of which are current in countries in West, East and Central Africa. Zambia is one of the countries that was rich in copper, which it exploited to the full with no reinvestment for diversification of the economy. A large consortium of quasi-government organisations was established which controlled all the mining companies and was managed by political nominees. It had a workforce of 29 000 people in a small country of under 7 million population. Because of operational inefficiencies the mammoth entity died a natural death within a decade, dragging its subsidiaries down with it. The national airline, once one of the best on the continent, ground to a halt with an embarrassing diplomatic incident involving the head of state. He had flown to England with the last plane in the fleet and it was attached by creditors. He was stranded until diplomatic shuttles led to the temporary release of the plane.

The second event concerns the national airline in Zimbabwe, where the tradition was to appoint chief executives on the strength of their political connections, disregarding business leadership experience and expertise. Consequently, successive incumbents did their part to run down the organisation. In the process one incumbent was dismissed for flagrantly bad management breaching the fundamentals of business ethics. The board of directors, who were also politically appointed and thus just as ineffective, bungled the dismissal by flouting legal procedures. Paradoxically, the chair was a lawyer of many years' experience. The dismissal remained abortive for three years while the individual earned his very generous package. In that period another CEO was appointed to run the firm. In effect, this small, loss-making airline had two chief executives for over two years. It demands these questions: Could the airline afford it? Why was such an inept board not fired immediately? How badly has service to the end customer been affected by this unprofessional managerial dysfunction? The answer to the last question is glaringly evident in poor staff morale, substandard airline service and low patronage with customers fleeing to competitors.

Yet another incident in the same country involved a chief executive of a national grain-marketing corporation who was dismissed for poor food security planning. He allegedly exported maize during a period of drought, resulting in the country importing maize in the end. The paradox of the situation was that he reported to a board and to the relevant government minister. A few months later, the incumbent was paid a severance sum of nearly two million in the local currency, which was a comfortable figure.

Who has suffered in all these cases of poor service? The list is endless, embracing the defenceless ordinary person, the already overburdened taxpayer and generally all the millions of customers whose needs would have been satisfied directly or indirectly if these parastatals had performed at optimum level and not collapsed.

As an integral aspect of the African Renaissance there are feasible moves towards privatisation of parastatals in several countries. This is a significant effort to convert the dinosaurs into manageable, transparent and efficient business units. Without the guaranteed funds from national coffers these right-sized organisations quickly learn to identify their customers, their needs and work to satisfy them. In this process the customer is much more likely to receive good service, which may be unknown in a parastatal environment.

Success stories of privatisation are often related about Ghana, Uganda and Zambia, while South Africa had also made good progress. These countries have made a bold move to sell off government ownership of parastatal organisations either wholly or through majority equity. The motivation is to release state assets into private business, which will maximise their profitability and minimise the need for government subsidies to sustain failing enterprises. The rationale is simply that government must be preoccupied with governing and leave business in the hands of expert business people. This way a win-win formula prevails for the benefit of the country.

A few countries such as Zimbabwe have been half-hearted about it by first becoming commercialised as a stopgap measure before privatisation. This entails floating enterprises on the stock exchange to open them up to the public in part while government is still in control. This tends to yield suboptimal results which will not relieve the national fiscus of the burden of subsidy if performance is negative. In essence, the enterprise remains public oriented in culture with a poor customer-care approach. Thus, it cannot compete effectively with a completely private business.

ABSOLUTE POWER NEGATES SERVICE EXCELLENCE

The history of most African countries is such that when they gained political independence they inherited large public service structures and limited private sector infrastructure. In the majority of cases public service had been used as an instrument for indoctrination and oppression of the society. Therefore, when revolution took place and overturned the power balance, the new regimes used the same infrastructure to effect change in the lives of the ordinary people. Thus, instead of less, it became more government, with total control on society. This is not the platform to weigh the pros and cons, but merely to emphasise the vital role played by the public sector in shaping its society positively or negatively. Indeed it is its role to dispense government service to the populace, which makes it a crucial instrument for customer service, or lack of it.

In nations where poverty is rampant and earning capacity limited, there is tremendous pressure on the public sector to be the provider for the nation. This turns it into a political vanguard by default as employees become subjected to political direction. They also seek to create their own wealth by exploiting the situation of scarcity. Society in general ceases to view the public servant as its servant but as an exalted provider of badly needed service. This breeds corruption as the public official now seeks to become elitist in line with societal expectations when in fact his or her income level is much lower. There are many countries on the continent where most brand-new cars are owned by politicians and public servants because they are the only ones with the means. This is a dangerous precedent because it spells economic disaster. Public service should only be a dispenser of service and not a creator of wealth. When the latter prevails, it means national resources are being channelled to the non-productive sector at the expense of productive investment. Among other follies this means service excellence to the people has been undermined by corruption and self-enrichment.

The following chronicle of events should illustrate the deep-seated culture of poor service and confusion between politics and public service. In private enterprise, service excellence is ensured by systematic coordination of all departments to fulfil one mission. This cohesion does not always exist in the public sector.

In our cities the institution of the mayor was inherited from the Western colonial powers but has been modified in different countries. Originally, it symbolised the city father who sought to upgrade the civic life of ratepayers. He was elected at set intervals and earned a nominal allowance for civic representation. The position was an elected one to ensure the incumbent had the mandate of his constituency and was fully knowledgeable of the needs of the community, which is his customer base.

In a few countries the position has become an executive and permanent one. This has created a host of problems. In Zimbabwe the mayoral elections became so politicised that only well-connected political parrots ever came into office. If an independent won the elections, they would have been rigged to the desired result. It needs no imagination to see that it was not the most competent candidate who got the job. Furthermore, by making the position permanent, sensitivity to customer needs was eliminated. The incumbent became his or her own master with no need for a mandate from the community. This was a recipe for corruption and inefficiency. In this particular case this has been fulfilled. The mayor became an extension of a corrupt political system and made the city insolvent within three years. A serious shortage of critical services prevailed in all parts of the city. The community became helpless because it could not kick him out. Paradoxically, the same community, under political direction, had voted for this candidate. Together with his councillors, he draws a huge monthly salary instead of the nominal allowance which symbolised only civic commitment. Gone is the orientation towards serving customers. In 1999 the government succumbed to societal pressure and dismissed the mayor with his entire executive management in a bid to salvage the pieces.

In Kenya a shameless debâcle about a radio licence took place, involving a private media company and officials of the Ministry of Communications. The media firm applied to the ministry for a radio broadcasting licence. The officials, acting under direction from the President's Office, did not respond for four years. The company proceeded to buy a 90% shareholding from an individual who had been granted a licence, but had no money to realise the project, which required millions of dollars. One may ask what business plan he had presented to the ministry to obtain a licence for national coverage without even start-up capital. When the ministry saw the transaction had been concluded, it unilaterally withdrew the licence. However, the company was now under different ownership with legal protection. A protracted legal battle ensued which the company won. As if that was not enough, the ministry then refused to grant it radio frequency authority. Another legal wrangle followed whose verdict is yet to be known.

Let us analyse this incident from the standpoint of service excellence. It became clear that government did not want to issue a radio licence to this firm for fear of it becoming too strong a critical machine against government as the company also owned a major newspaper. Instead, it felt comfortable about granting numerous regional licences to small applicants who were not likely to make them operational in a meaningful way. This was a ploy to deflect criticism by the citizens that government refused to grant licences. Public servants in the Ministry of Communication were serving only themselves and their political masters. You cannot give differential treatment to a range of customers seeking the same service. In this instance the public service machinery was turned from a service provider to a service regulator. Needless to say, this runs completely against the grain of service excellence. Yet it is prevalent in many countries.

Another example of the institutionalised practice of self-service by public servants, which can be construed as corruption at its worst, occurred in Swaziland, Zimbabwe, Lesotho and other countries in Central Africa. Several financial donors, including governments from the West, pledged educational scholarships to those African countries which had previously been their colonies or were seen as being in dire need. The aid funds were and still are administered by government ministries. An open system of selection of beneficiaries is supposed to take place where the most deserving or the best student should obtain a scholarship to study outside the home country. Invariably, applications have been manipulated to the extent that mainly the children of the public servants and their immediate relatives obtained them. In one country the majority of students who went to study overseas shared only two surnames, those of leading families in society. Even more distressingly, the selected candidates are not the most academically gifted, which means they have to repeat several years, consuming more money in the process and still returning home as mediocre performers. Through such practice the public service has short-changed its society and compromised future national performance. Should access to service depend on whom you know in the system?

High-profile cases of abuse of power for personal gain are commonplace in many of our countries. A synopsis of some of them may help to show the disturbing prevalence of such underhand behaviour among those in leadership. In the late 1980s four Zimbabwean Cabinet Ministers were compelled to leave in disgrace over a scandal of buying motor cars from a government-controlled assembly plant and re-selling at exorbitant prices, taking advantage of the chronic mid-nineties shortage of cars in the country. In the mid-nineties Zambia also witnessed embarrassing cases of corruption at Cabinet level. The first democratic government of South Africa was embarrassed when a Cabinet Minister was prosecuted for irregularities in disbursing social welfare funds for pensioners. He had to resign under a cloud. Most recently a director-general in the Department of Home Affairs was relieved of his post for gross misconduct involving issuing false identity documents and citizenship to foreigners for personal gain, running a private business from a government office, paying own domestic staff with state funds, and abuse of state vehicles for private business errands. In Swaziland a state-owned financial institution had to be rescued from bankruptcy by the government when the chief executive overexposed its lending to politicians and members of the royal clan. He sacrificed the business for his personal political ambitions, as he shortly afterwards campaigned for a parliamentary seat. Also in 1999 the head of the Lesotho Highlands Water Authority faced public accusations of corruption in awarding tenders to suppliers of materials during the construction of the multi-million dollar project. The negative publicity which ensued caused international embarrassment as names of certain financiers and donor countries were dragged into the fray. Most recently, newspapers carried an embarrassing story of a top ministerial official in Nigeria who sold state land to the government, claiming it was his. The newly elected president, Obasanjo, has vowed to eradicate corruption, which is widely regarded as a cancer eating into the entire fabric of the business and economic society of this most populous country in Africa.

The parastatals are vital components of public service. These are business institutions which are supposed to add to and not deplete the national fiscus. Originally established to safeguard and ensure equitable distribution of strategic national services such as electricity, railways, airways, information broadcasting and agricultural marketing, they have been turned into political weaponry operated by public servants manipulated by politicians.

In many countries, chief executives of these parastatals are failed civil servants or politicians dumped there as rewards for loyalty. It is believed that they will be less embarrassing in that position. On the contrary, they tend to cost the nation dearly because of mismanagement. Quite often the board of directors is composed of hand-picked sycophants of the ruling party whose knowledge of business is dangerous. As a result, many airlines have closed down, railways are permanently subsidised, agricultural marketing authorities have increased starvation because of lack of planning, and the taxpayer always pays the price.

In Zimbabwe a public servant was appointed to head a reasonably strong bank in which government has majority equity. Within three years the bank was on the brink of bankruptcy because of mismanagement. Another quasi-government body had a fascinating case of a board of directors who voted themselves huge salaries while the parastatal was bleeding with losses. They were asked to stand down to give way to a privatisation programme, but they refused until legal force was used. In

South Africa, directors individually and collectively instructed the payroll department of their employer parastatal to award them twice the bonus passed by board resolution. They just felt they needed more. By the way, some of these boards comprised people of all races, which proves that misdemeanours know no colour.

What observations can be made in all these cases? First, management is a profession in its own right that takes years to master. A good politician or public servant does not necessarily become a good business manager. The entire society would receive the service it deserved if good politicians remained in politics and public service, while competent business managers were left to run the parastatals unhindered. Second, all those involved in these incidents were serving only themselves. Public servants must be given to a measure of selflessness. They must be trained to exhibit an attitude of doing something good in the national interest and not personal appeasement. Third, politicians breed corruption in public service by interfering with administration. Politics should remain in the legislature and the constituency (local or national), while public service is the executive arm of government run professionally to implement the statutes of the land without fear or favour. Only then can the ordinary person begin to receive service excellence.

Customer service training works wonders in the private sector. It should be implemented with the same vigour in the public sector. Although a tremendous amount of training occurs in this sector, it is designed mainly to upgrade technical and administrative skills. It hardly ever attends to behavioural competences which improve understanding of people, managing personal behaviour and inculcating passion for giving service in the line of duty.

It is some consolation that lack of service orientation in public service is not confined to Africa. I and many others have suffered humiliation at the hands of immigration and customs officials at airports in Britain, USA and New Zealand. You would be pulled out of the line of passengers arriving from Africa. As you are asked to put your bags on a table you realise that all the others at the table are mainly African people (and orientals in USA), which immediately tells you that the public servant manning that gate has been indoctrinated to assume fault in any person of colour. The humiliation and frustration are often aggravated because the official will unceremoniously empty your suitcase, leaving all your personal belongings scattered on the workbench. When inevitably they do not find what they are looking for, they move off without a word and you must re-pack your bags.

Ingrained bias in the staff against people of a certain description causes them not to wish to serve them as equal customers. Instead they are viewed as mere numbers passing through the terminal. Airports are the gateways into a country and impressions formed by a visitor there will shape his or her attitude towards the country for a long time in future. Therefore, some of this behaviour has probably damaged national images irreparably.

On a positive note there are abundant cases of service excellence to be cited from public institutions at home and abroad. Even more customer-oriented are some African government departments which have formulated mission statements which are displayed boldly in the offices. I recall that a couple of years ago in South Africa, I received a phone call from a government clerical official to follow up on a problem that I had presented to his department the week before. He wanted to know if I had received help from where his office referred me to. This gave me a lot of hope that society may still receive efficient service from the public service with no strings attached. I will continue to support the efforts to create service excellence awareness by our public servants.

Some governments have taken the bold step of drawing skills from the private into public sector. With increasing frequency one sees political leaders co-opting eminent business people or academics to senior Cabinet posts in their areas of expertise. Such developments help to create a business climate with a service culture brought by the leader from his or her experience. An added advantage is that professional managers are not susceptible to nepotism and they have a strategic view of the business.

To monitor service levels rendered to society by the public sector, some governments, such as South Africa, have established temporary or permanent watchdog agencies. These include police complaints directorates, public service commissions, government-funded consumer protection councils, anti-corruption units and the office of the public protector. In an effort to satisfy foreign investment customers, several countries have established national investment centres as integrated sources of ready information for potential investors. This can be a most positive and effective way of meeting the needs of several categories of customers as well as raising the international profile of the country. In Uganda I was delighted to see a clearly business-oriented attitude in public servants. They met me at my hotel over a weekend to supply me with investment information. Similarly, I found it much easier to meet with heads of government in Uganda, Swaziland and Lesotho than in some countries. There seems to be some correlation between government openness and service excellence.

Let us close with some international parallels. One that comes to mind immediately is the Singapore Immigration and Tourism Department. If you pass through Changhi International Airport in transit you are permitted to go into the city without a visa. You leave your passport at immigration, embark on a free bus supplied for the purpose, and you are taken on a three-hour guided tour of Singapore. You collect your passport on return, and you are invariably full of praise for their beautiful and clean city. This is an example of a public service sector making an additional effort to please customers who are passing through, with the ultimate goal of promoting the city image for tourism. With good leadership training and commitment the public sector can become a most effective dispenser of service excellence.

SERVICE THROUGH VALUE-ADDING

The preceding critical analysis of lack of customer sensitivity in the public sector was not intended as a blanket damning report. There are ample opportunities for making tangible improvements in all aspects of public

83

activity. However, it entails a whole paradigm shift for leadership, employees and the recipients of the service.

The business sector is fundamentally different from other endeavours because of the profit motive, or the aim to multiply whatever commodity was initially invested. The same concept can be introduced in the public sector, with modifications. Let us take a typical government department staffed by typical civil servants. How can the profit motive be implemented? I believe that if politicians removed themselves from managing the operating departments and left this to the principal secretary as chief executive, that would be a good beginning. The latter would be asked to produce an operating annual business plan to the treasury to motivate for funds. Once granted, it becomes his or her total responsibility to utilise those funds correctly, and prove this in an annual report to the public. If he or she fails to meet the objectives for which money was granted, he or she should bear the same consequences as the chief executive in the private sector – be fired.

By the same token, if the department utilises its funds so well that it meets its operational plan and still retains savings which have not arisen from starving the public of needed services, it should be allowed to keep this money for further utilisation, including rewarding high-performing staff. Once staff see that there is a rigorous performance management system which sets goals in terms of quality and quantity of service dispensed, and consistently measures it, as a result of which reward and punishment are meted out, they would find reason to meet the needs of their customers.

For instance, why should public offices all open and close at the same time throughout the country although public requirements may be different. Imagine the positive impact it would make if government departments worked shifts, so that even after work one could still go to the nearest office and get the required service. The same principle can be applied to local authorities and municipal offices. In this way public servants would be adding value to their ordinary efforts to give their customer the advantage of availability, utility and applicability of service.

Recently I was most frustrated by lack of service when I made a long cross-border trip and went with my father to the local district government office to transfer land ownership from him to me. Only one person deals with that and he was on holiday. I now have to wait for another year to find the time to make such a trip again.

In the same way, municipal and parastatal workers can be mobilised to believe that they are running their own strategic business unit from whose success they benefit and whose failure results in material deprivation. Salary increases and promotion should not be based on how long one has been in the organisation but how well one performs. Similarly, the infamous thirteenth cheque bonus should be replaced by a performance-related bonus which separates poor and high performers. Quite often in hotels and other public-oriented enterprises we are given service questionnaires to complete which are scrutinised by relevant authorities to effect service improvements. Public sector departments should have such performance measures to give us the opportunity to evaluate the service received from an organisation or even an individual employee. If I can report a vehicle driver who is driving recklessly to his superior through a phone number on the back of the vehicle, why should I not be able to do the same with an employee who is paid with my tax money and who denies me service?

In simplistic terms it has been demonstrated that if public sector departments were to be incentivised to increase their accountability to the public they would feel compelled to give impeccable service. If there is something in it for employees they would go the extra mile to please their customers. Such extra effort draws a distinction between service excellence and poor careless inaction from those whose behaviour influences society enormously.

A DOZEN TECHNIQUES FOR CULTURE CHANGE

What is required to infuse a new way of behaving and managing into quasi-public organisations? A complete about-turn is imperative in all involved including the political players who pull the power strings. In practice a new culture should prevail to influence new thinking, introduce new leadership practices and inspire high organisational productivity. To drive this point home let us familiarise ourselves with the dozen techniques of building a new service-oriented culture in an organisation.

- **Clarity:** *The change facilitators must be absolutely clear about what needs to be changed. It should be clear whether it is the structure or systems or strategy for service delivery. The time frame and deadlines for change should be delineated as well as the way in which it will be achieved. This should be simply expressed in words such as competitive threat, cost escalation and such-like business jargon, which all can understand. The modalities of doing it and necessary resources should be spelt out. Make it come alive! Use metaphors, symbols, slogans and pictures. Do not confuse the message, but create a picture or vision of how things will be after the change. In other words, all involved must be made to share the vision of the ultimate cathedral to be built by the sum total of the incremental efforts of each of them.*

- **Consistency:** *There should be perseverence and focus towards the goal. Stick to it and do not succumb to inconsistency. A big ship takes time to turn, and this holds true of culture change. It took three years to effect a turnaround in Jaguar's quality, some five years for complete culture change in British Airways, and Citicorp took three years for a full market repositioning.*

- **Context:** *Change does not occur in a vacuum but within an established context of time and space. There should be no need for zero-based change. Instead, it should be formulated to fit into the existing context. Exploit strategic synergies by connecting what you want to achieve with things that others want to achieve. Position it optimally to decide which existing aspects fit into the new order. This requires an astute scanning of the total environment in which change will take place.*

- **Teamwork:** *You cannot change an organisation alone, so it is advisable to marshall the support and commitment of all relevant people. Coordinate your* *efforts with other team members to gain critical mass for change. Remember: 'Lone hero innovators are usually martyred.'*

- **Opinion leaders:** *Identify real champions of the idea of change, whom others will follow. These can be drawn from people in powerful positions and those with demonstrable energy. Champions have the tenacity to cope with ambiguity, uncertain circumstances, complexity and change.*

- **Planned communication:** *Tell the world about success stories and the runner-up processes followed. It is more advantageous to use multifaceted communication media including the grapevine machinery. Each stage of change must be surrounded by ample communication about it.*

- **Dedication and passion:** *Do not embark on change if people at the top only display lukewarm support. They should show total commitment to change – psychologically, physically and intellectually. Transformational leaders such as Lee Iacocca of Chrysler, Welch of General Electric, Egan of Jaguar, Marshall of British Airways and Harvey-Jones of ICI believed in what they were doing and worked tirelessly to achieve it. They had vision and a passion for service excellence.*

- **Orchestration of good news:** *Use every opportunity and excuse to celebrate small successes. The process of change should radiate a spirit of fun to attract others to join and help. Celebrations are sources of motivation for those in the firing line who may succumb to fatigue.*

- **Smart partnerships:** *Build coalitions with other groups and departments who aspire to the same future state of change. It is immaterial what their reasons are as long as they share a similar desire for change in the same area. There is both wisdom and safety from risk in a group approach.*

- **Consequences:** *Have some built-in assessment process which will detect the consequences and knock-on effects of your change efforts. Change in one area tends to have ripple effects on a distant part of the system. These consequences need to be managed carefully.*

- **Consolidate:** *Cement the change into the fabric of the organisation to make it a normal part of life. Once it is institutionalised, move onto the next stage* to a permanent state of affairs. Disband the ad hoc arrangements originally set up to implement the change.

- **Enduring courage:** *The boldness of the leader of the top team to drive the initiative through is vital for lasting success. Transformational leadership which is dedicated to a values-driven fundamental change is more lasting than transactional leadership in which the daily transactions of the business are well managed but subject to blowing with the corporate wind.*

The common thread running through this entire culture change strategy is 'people', especially those who manage the customer's experience. They are key assets who either make the change initiative succeed or fail to make a positive impact on the external customer.

Chapter 5

Service or not in the professions

A working definition of the field of professions would be a good start for our discussion. This term is used to collectively describe those fields of work in which performers are guided by a code of behaviour and knowledge resulting from a defined international qualification. The code of behaviour also denotes internationally recognised ethics and expectations. The most commonly known professions are the following:

- *the accounting profession, which is guided by GAAP (generally accepted accounting principles)*
- *the medical profession, which is bound by a very stringent code of ethics embodied in the medical professional councils of various countries*
- *the psychological profession, which has a code of behaviour centred on confidentiality*
- *social work, whose five fundamental principles emphasise the helping nature of the endeavour*
- *the legal profession, which also has a stringent code of ethics espoused by various law societies*
- *the educational profession, which follows similar trends*
- *management in general, one of the most pervasive professions in our daily lives*
- *a host of technical professions including engineering, architecture and the whole range of scientific professions.*

It is indisputable that together the professions control societal behaviour to the extent that right and wrong are based on them as a frame of reference. Similarly, it follows that they play a pivotal role in customer service or lack of it within society as a whole and its sectional groupings. This is more so because most professions have assembled into large

89

collective bodies such as the Law Society, Medical Professions Council, and educationists' associations.

THE PROFESSIONAL SERVICE VILLAINS

The next chronicle of events represents neglect or total lack of service orientation on the part of the professional people involved.

Anecdote 1
This happened to me a couple of years ago in South Africa and to three other people I know in Swaziland, Zimbabwe and South Africa in the last ten years. It is now mandatory to be tested for the HIV virus if you approach a financial institution to borrow a large sum of money for investment in a project such as house purchase, for which insurance cover is required. A strict procedural code has been sanctioned by the World Health Organisation to regulate the conducting of tests. Its fundamental tenet is that before the test the incumbent must be counselled by a qualified professional or doctor on the implications of the test and possible repercussions. This is designed to pre-empt trauma in the event of the test proving positive. In none of the above cases did this happen. I recall being given a laboratory form to complete at reception where I was given the test form to take to the laboratory. On arriving at the laboratory where I expected a semblance of counselling, a blood sample was taken and I was told the results will be given to me by the doctor within two days. This did not happen and after three weeks I called my bank. Only then did I learn that all had gone well and the insurance policy had been granted. My other two colleagues had similar experiences elsewhere. Here is a simple analysis of the service sabotage action. First, failure to prepare the incumbent for possible devastating results is very unprofessional. Second, not advising of the results at all when a feedback time frame of two days had been given is almost criminal.

Anecdote 2

Two years ago a friend had to go into one of the top private hospitals in South Africa for some medical scanning. She was asked to undress and wear a hospital gown. For some 45 minutes she stood in the wide corridor without being attended to. This was in the middle of winter. Then she was ushered into the room where the scanning was conducted swiftly and she was left alone without a word as to what to do next. After nearly one hour she came out and found that all the staff for that section had gone home. She had to phone the following morning to find out the results. The nurse answered thus: 'It seems something was found, you may need to come back.' The patient wrote a strong complaint letter to the managing director of the hospital group but received no answer.

It can correctly be pointed out that the entire private hospital was anti-customer service, including the managing director, as he saw no need to reply to the letter. This happens so frequently that society now subconsciously accepts it and hence perpetuates the malpractice.

Anecdote 3

Another patient went into a reputable hospital in South Africa for a major operation. He had been admitted by a surgeon of some standing who did not prepare him with professional advance care, except to tell him the place, the date and time of hospitalisation. When the patient arrived to check into the ward, only then was he told that the costs for the first three days were to be paid in cash up-front and not as part of the medical aid bill. Here was a severely sick person, covered by medical aid, but being told at the last minute that he must pay up thousands of rands at his bedside. Fortunately a friend who had taken him paid by credit card and the operation went ahead.

The gripe here is not that inhuman treatment was meted out to this patient. It is simply a matter of customer care on the part of the surgeon. He should have a simple advisory system in place to brief would-be patients well enough for them to be prepared. A person in emotional trauma needs that so much more than I do when I go to buy a used car. Yet in the latter case the salesman spends time explaining the features of the car to the customer.

Anecdote 4

Before the same patient checked into the ward, he had asked about house rules regarding personal care items. The answer was 'Just pack an overnight bag.' The patient specifically asked whether soap and towels were to be included but was told they were. He went into the ward only to experience the opposite and had to start calling for help from friends. That is not easy when you are in intensive care. Again, this is a simple matter of supplying a customer with relevant information. Surely, this is not too much to ask of any professional who trained for years at college.

Anecdote 5

Sexually biased management

For many years I heard about carpet interviews but never took them seriously, probably because I was in the field of employment and could not imagine interviewing in any way other than the professional four-stage procedure. One day a friend rang me up almost speechless with anger. She had been called for an interview at an agency for a professional position. On arrival she was ushered into the office of this big man (in size). He came round the desk to sit on the same side. She did not panic because this falls within the ambit of modern-day interviewing without formal barriers. The interview degenerated into a probe into her social life and she became uneasy, but decided to be patient. But the man began explicitly flirting with her, at which stage she stormed out in disgust. Her first question to me was: 'Is this what you do all the time?' Obviously it took me time and effort to explain that this style does not exist in textbooks on professional interviewing.

This behaviour falls into the categories of sexual harassment and so-called carpet interviews. A job applicant comes for an interview with high expectations of a fair discussion, information on the firm and, it is hoped, a job at the end. If he or she is suddenly confronted with other personal demands, that person obviously feels devastated and let down by lack of professionalism. To show how revolting it can be I asked one colleague who I knew was prone to such behaviour what he would do if the same was done to his wife or sister. The answer was quick and unequivocal: 'I will kill somebody.' One of the principles of service excellence is the biblical adage that 'You do unto others what you wish done unto you'. My colleague obviously needs to read the Old Testament again to learn excellent customer service.

Anecdote 6
Management by bottom power
The preceding observation dwelt on the seemingly helpless female species being harassed by shameless male predators. Let us look at the flip side of the coin where some women wield tremendous power over their male counterparts by virtue of sexual blackmail. In one Central African country a powerful female business executive got what she wanted in every respect from any of her male subordinates, superiors and counterparts through her unique power of overnight persuasion. She would order a male subordinate to come to her house at night for some work which was never publicly defined. The end result was a polarisation of relations between male and female staff that seriously hampered its delivery of service to the customers. Staff promotions were based on arbitrary sexual grounds instead of merit, which led to inefficiency and disgruntlement among the more able staff who were bypassed.

Thus service excellence was undermined by this bottom power behaviour to very far-reaching proportions. Think how many times this has happened in situations you know about. The answer probably will be 'many times over'. Then ask yourself: 'Is it possible to display both favouritism and fairness at the same time?' This type of arbitrary behaviour militates against service excellence from every angle. You cannot have your cake and eat it.

Anecdote 7

One of the most gruesome cases in the medical profession happened a few years ago in Zimbabwe, resulting in a jail sentence for an anaesthetist on two counts of manslaughter. He had indulged in the diabolical malpractice of experimenting on black patients with different concoctions of anaesthetic drugs. As a result, two people died, causing a major public outrage, which quickly took on racial overtones of unimaginable proportions. A protracted legal suit ensued which culminated in imprisonment, which is seen by some public observers as too light for the crime. Apart from the heinous crime of racial discrimination, this person had betrayed the sanctity of the medical profession. Professionals cannot subject their customers to dangerous experiments, particularly without their consent. In this case these patients were customers in a commercial and in a professional sense. He failed to uphold either of these service principles.

THE SERVICE GAP

This denotes the discord that prevails when the expectations or perceptions of delivery action fall short of what the recipient actually experiences inthe relative context. The latter qualifying phrase emphasises the reasonableness and relevance of the expectations. For instance, it would be sheer folly for one to expect the same smooth ride in a Volkswagen Beetle as in a Mercedes Benz. Therefore if because of circumstances only the former vehicle is available, this does not ipso facto constitute poor service, provided all care is accorded to the customer. Every time that you left a place disgruntled, picked a squabble with the taxi driver, disagreed with your boss, or signed a petition against your local community leader, you were reacting against a service gap which you experienced. The question is 'How does one fill the gap?' However, effective cure follows good diagnosis of the cause of symptoms of the disease manifested by the service gap. The following is a short list of variables which sometimes impact on service providers in the various professions analysed earlier.

- **Level of sophistication:** *Some professionals tend to become too sophisticated to really understand their customers. Consequently they will not stop to understand their needs, but only see their own aspirations as the key drivers for action. You cannot effectively serve people to whom you have a condescending attitude. No service excellence can be given to the slave by the master, only benevolent dictatorship.*

- **Present and historical understanding:** *If someone does not have in-depth knowledge and understanding of service circumstances, he or she is likely to render tardy service. Most environmental and demographic trends change in quantum leaps in Africa because of the technological influence of the donor super powers. Some professionals fail to keep abreast of changes, which compounds lack of understanding.*

- **Learning capacity:** *It is forgivable to give poor service because of genuine ignorance but unforgivable to do so deliberately. This is often the cardinal error of the ostrich mentality where one believes that by burying one's head in the sand the challenges of the surroundings will disappear. Some professional people cease to learn from the day they finish training and cannot see the wood for the trees throughout their working life thereafter.*

- **Stigma attached to the situation:** *Those who believe their professional status is high tend to become class conscious about those they deal with. Similarly those of lower achievement, but who mistakenly believe they have arrived, will tend to lack customer care and professional approach.*

- **Clash of professional values and business expediency:** *In the early eighties I had two acquaintances who qualified as medical doctors in a country with a dire shortage of such skills. They had hardly practised in public hospitals when they opened several private practices, which they openly referred to as 'shops'. Clearly, professional care for patients was compromised for business expediency.*

- **Inherent mediocrity in society:** *The public, who are on the receiving end of service, should be the most potent watchdog against substandard treatment by the professions. Unfortunately, the African spirit of respect bequeathed us a legacy of docile acceptance of mediocre standards without rejection or complaint. As a result, poor service becomes a self-fulfilling prophecy. By the way, this shortfall seems to affect everyone who lives in Africa, irrespective of colour.*

THE TEN COMMANDMENTS FOR SERVICE EXCELLENCE

More than other members of society, professionals are judged very strictly by on-lookers and recipients of their service. This is understandable since their behaviour impacts on the soul of the society more than other walks of life. Second, it is easier to measure professional conduct against international benchmarks. In the wake of such high expectations there ought to be a generic frame of reference for all professional service providers. To initiate the debate, I outline ten non-negotiable command-ments which apply across the spectrum.

1   *All professionals and their lieutenants should be adequately service-oriented to realise that a customer is the most important visitor they receive at any time in their work period. Some professions do not even have defined work periods, which makes service alertness a round-the-clock phenomenon. Often one visits firms of lawyers, doctors' surgeries, architects' offices and many other professionals to be confronted with a prominent sign which reads 'Business hours 08h00 to 13h00; 13h00 to 14h00 lunch; 14h00 to16h30'. This lunchtime is designed for the convenience of the person who is supposed to attend to customers and not for the latter. In plain language the message is 'Customer, wait. I will help you when it is convenient to me'. By implication, the customer is viewed as a disturbance of peace, whose nuisance value is considerable.*

2   *The customer comes first at all times. Professionals have to inculcate the six skills represented by the following acronym (adapted from Hopson & Scally 1989) to facilitate rote memory. 'Comes first' stands for:*

C = clear messages
O = OK attitude
M = making people feel special
E = energy
S = service under pressure

First = the first four minutes and last two minutes

To render professional service in any discipline one must have the above basic people skills. These refer to communicating clear messages; demonstrating a positive attitude at all times, making everyone feel special, showing high energy and giving consistent service under pressure. Remember that customers are not idiots, they always know when they are not welcome, no matter how well disguised the behaviour is.

3   *The customer is not dependent on you. You are dependent on the customer, whether he or she is a patient, a legal client, a prisoner, a school pupil or a passenger in transit. In everyday life we have seen schools close down because there were no pupils to make them sustainable. Therefore, teachers have lost employment or been re-deployed to where there is a need for their services. Similarly, there have been occasions when public offices closed down because of lack of patronage by people who require the services rendered there. In the private sector the equation is extremely straightforward – no customers, no business.*

4   *A customer is not an interruption to your work; he or she is the cause of it. Customers are evaluating your performance in handling them. From this evaluation strong opinions arise that can be positive or negative towards the professional person. When you are serving a customer, whether as a teacher, doctor, nurse, policeman, lawyer, business manager,*

banker or any other profession, you are on stage. The questions you should answer upfront are: Are you dressed for the part? Do you know your lines? Do you understand the play?

5	The customer is not an outsider in your organisation but an important partner. Those organisations which have constant open communication with their customers are the market leaders because they know what their customers want, and when and how they want it before producing it. During hard times customers stick to those businesses which gave them respect by asking their opinion and shared consumer plans with them.

6	Remember that when a customer calls on your services you are not doing him or her a favour, although the opposite is true. By seeking your services the customer is giving you a vote of confidence which you should seize eagerly to prove your ounce of gold. The logic is simple and straightforward if the professional views it this way – if this individual, and many others, did not seek your services as a doctor, lawyer, policeman, accountant, manager, nurse and so forth, you would be redundant.

7	The corollary to this principle is that customers do not owe you anything by seeking your services. They can go elsewhere if they are not satisfied with you. When resources are scarce, short-sighted service providers foolishly believe that they are the only ones capable of meeting the customers' needs and they have no alternative. This is tantamount to shooting oneself in the foot because once an option presents itself, even second rate in service, customers will change allegiance overnight, if only out of spite. Many enterprises have gone bust unexpectedly through this invincible power of consumers.

8	Every person who renders service to others, at whatever level this may be, must remember that the first four minutes of the encounter are critical and the last two minutes are crucial for a sustainable service relationship.

In the first four minutes you are the organisation you work for. When customers interact with you they are doing so with the full conviction that you are the organisation. If you captivate customers by radiating understanding of other needs, willingness to satisfy them and taking an appropriate timely action you have created a memorable customer experience. That will become your individual credit, which will ensure they do not go to competition.

The last two minutes are crucial because the first impression lingers longest after the event. Your concluding behaviour sets the tone for the moment of truth that you have just had with the customer. Create a professional but warm and personal image capped by a definite indication of action.

It is important to remember that at every moment of truth there are three possible customer behaviours:

- Customers will get less than they expect and be disappointed or angry (ie the service is memorable because it is horrible)
- Customers will get exactly what they expect and therefore it is 'no big deal' (ie forgettable because it is natural!)
- Customers get service of a higher quality than they expect and are delighted (ie it is memorable because it's magic!) This is the eternal aim of service excellence.

9   In whatever capacity you may be operating, always remember the customer's bill of rights. Rule 1 is that the customer is always right, regardless of the circumstances. The onus is on professionals to navigate around potential conflict with the customer because they cannot win the argument. Rule 2 is that if you should find the customer wrong, return immediately to rule 1. Ultimately the customer is king. He or she is the reason for your being in the profession that you took.

10   Foster a relationship of mutual benefit which enables you to profit through service. The 80/20 rule dictates that under normal circumstances in a

market situation, professions included, 80% of business comes from 20% of the client base. This means people relationships are fundamental to success in service, which has led to conversion of the order of business' critical success factors. The traditional business approach was dominated by the pursuit of profit. Therefore the business philosophy was in this order:

- profit
- product
- people

The product came a natural second, being the chief source of profit. People came at the bottom of the scale because their only relevance and value was in terms of the first two elements. In organisations oriented towards service, the order has been turned:

- people
- product
- profit

The people who manage the customer's experience are key assets. They should be developed, encouraged, inspired and supported to empower them to deliver the service excellence, the quality product, which will make you profitable. All professional service providers should be convinced that investment in people is a central quality service requirement; it is not optional.

PROFIT THROUGH SERVICE

A comprehensive diagnosis of the service gap disease has been made. Can we now prescribe the medicine, whether in the form of a Western scientific prescription or an African spiritually inspired herbal medicine? Perhaps a combination would more effectively treat our cosmopolitan service providers.

First, our service-dispensing professionals should not view the call for world-class service as implying everything Western and nothing home-grown. A happy medium is the panacea which should be sought all the time. Technology per se does not render service excellence, but it facilitates that state if it is blended appropriately with the human element.

Second, dispensing good service to anyone must take some personal sacrifice or thought. If service is dished out in a mechanical fashion it will not pass the test of time. The concept of indoctrination is not far-fetched in this context. McDonalds does not export hamburgers around the world, but indoctrinates service dispensers with the philosophy of quality, service, cleanliness and value. In the same vein Japanese with their 'kaizen' (incremental improvement) imply the belief that every little step builds up to a quantum leap.

Finally, service excellence does not occur in a vacuum but must be predicated upon a strong supportive system. Part of it is teamwork, starting with as few people as two, such as a boss and secretary or a doctor and nurse. A supportive macro system is essential as well. An efficient political system gives rise to an effective public service which meets the society's needs.

THE WIN/WIN/WIN/WIN FORMULA

Customer service training equips people to add value to the products they sell. Irrespective of their level of sophistication and station in life, one needs to develop relationships with those in the capacity of customers of any form, beyond just selling a product or service. This applies equally within and outside the organisational entity. It starts from the premise that 'You don't have to be unwell to get better'. It encourages people to be more skilled and aware that they can enhance their jobs, their professional contribution and the customer's experience. It results in WIN/WIN/WIN/WIN outcomes. Who wins?

First, customers or clients win because they enjoy quality treatment. Second, service providers win by getting satisfaction from a job well done.

101

Third, the business wins as customers indulge in repeat-buys of the product/service and they advertise to others. The fourth winner is society! If quality treatment of people is to become the great concern of the business world, if it can be re-emphasised in the caring professions, in our education systems, in health and community services, in political movements, then there really must be hope for greater quality of life for us all.

SOME PROFESSIONAL SERVICE HEROES

A year ago I was spending some leisure time on the central beaches of Durban when I saw a man lying slumped on the ground not far from a food court which included some bars. It was clear the man was in a drunken stupor in the mid-afternoon. Outside one of the restaurants were two members of the police force sipping soft drinks. They saw the man simultaneously, finished their drinks in a hurry and approached him. On discovering his problem, they lifted him respectfully and helped him into the shade a hundred metres away, where he could sober up. This incident impressed me because the officers had no obligation to prop up inebriated beachcombers.

The second admirable story of professionalism before commercialism involves a medical doctor who has looked after me and my family for some years. I told him that my father was suffering from acute arthritis for which he needed relief. I described the symptoms to him as my father was several hundreds of kilometres away. He quickly identified the medicine, which is rather pricey. As he knew I was travelling to see my father he gave me a packet of tablets to give him. I asked how much they cost and his reply was: 'Let's see if they work well first.'

Yet another doctor friend of mine earned a sterling reputation amongst older patients. He did this by taking time to explain in detail what the person was suffering from, how it had been contracted and the possible cures. He would go as far as to explain how the prescribed medicine worked. The paradox was that even those who could not understand the scientific causality of ailments came out of his surgery beaming with new knowledge and seemingly got better. It was well-deserved reward for my friend when he was appointed to a top post for Africa in the World Health Organisation.

SERVICE EXCELLENCE IS ORDAINED OF GOD

In the Gospel of John chapter 13 the Lord Jesus sets a heavenly example of service excellence which has guided mankind for two millennia. After the Last Supper, before his betrayal and crucifixion, the teaching says: 'Jesus ... rose from supper and laid aside his garments, took a towel and girded himself. After that he poured water into a basin and began to wash the disciples' feet and to wipe them with the towel with which he was girded ... If I then, your Lord and Teacher, have washed your feet, you also ought to wash one another's feet.'

This teaching is highly symbolic in both the spiritual and customer service sense. Jesus wanted to leave his disciples with an unequivocal example of rendering service to others. He wanted them to create a multiplier effect of such service orientation from this lesson. It achieved tremendous success, as his teaching dominates the Christian faith today throughout the world. Even some professions with the basic tenet of caring for society, such as medicine and statecraft, include in their oath of practice something to do with carrying out the will of God. Hence the phrase 'So help me, God' at the end of the oath. Thus, the Lord himself ordained the act and philosophy of service excellence.

Chapter 6

Necessity for service-oriented community leadership

A community is a neighbourhood with certain common interests or concerns, although it does not necessarily have to be homogeneous. Examples include a municipal ward, district or rural council, political cell, village and localised associations such as those for employees or employers, church congregation and sporting and special interest groups. Similarly, community leadership refers to the elected or appointed torchbearers such as city mayors and councillors, political stewards, church and union officials. These leaders play a critical role in shaping society's opinion and definition of service excellence or disservice, since the larger society is an aggregate sum of the constituent communities.

The concept of community in certain African contexts presents some real challenges to the leadership. These range from historical economic imbalances, deprivation and the need to bridge the gap between the haves and have-nots through redistribution of resources. This emanates from the racially based geographical distribution of populations which was legally instituted when the countries were first settled by the white people. Consequently, you find that in many African cities the well-serviced low-density suburbs were demarcated for whites and the deprived and overcrowded high-density townships were for black people. Similarly, life outside the cities was divided racially into commercial areas with land title deeds for whites and national land or tribal trust land for blacks. These demarcations were enshrined in such laws as Group Areas Act in South Africa, and Land Apportionment Act and Land Tenure Act in most former British colonies on the continent. The imbalances emanating from such artificial settlements became an economic reality in that the one side was affluent while the other was deprived of resources. In these circumstances the community leaders in the latter areas battle to serve their customers without the adequate facilities to do this. Consequently, it may be difficult for customers to experience satisfaction most of the time.

Be that as it may, reality dictates that unequal circumstances are a fact of life irrespective of whether it is in the eurocentric or afrocentric environment. Therefore, evaluation of service effectiveness must be relative to the community concerned. However, a service-oriented attitude in all leaders is a prerequisite. For this reason I enumerate the leadership qualities that are vital for effective community service.

- **Selflessness and commitment:** *An effective leader must display a notable element of sacrifice of something important to him or her and others. This could be forfeiting personal time, freedom, comfort and so forth. The motivation for sacrifice is rooted in commitment to a cause which may be elusive in the minds of the community folk. A case in point is that of most political leaders in pre-independence African countries who risked being imprisoned or having to live in exile for the cause of freedom for their nation. In most cases the freedom was very elusive but their spirit of sacrifice made it a reality in the end. A real leader does things for the common good without saying 'What's in it for me?' Satisfaction should come from winning the war and not a series of battles.*

- **Conceptualisation of reality:** *Community needs often involve blurred definitions of an aggregate of problems ranging from basic infrastructure to sophisticated state-of-the-art electronic equipment of any form. A good leader has the ability to conceptualise reality from an imperfect state of affairs to delineate the possible from the ideal. This includes prioritising community problems, separating necessities from the nice-to-haves.*

- **Motivation and mobilisation of masses:** *Having conceptualised reality, a leader must then define a superordinate common goal with which every community member will identify. This becomes the source of motivation to spur all and sundry into action. This requires sharpened skills of* perceptiveness and decisiveness. One must be relentless in pursuit of the goal and lead prominently by encouraging participation of all members. This is why demonstrations and mass rallies play an important role in our communities in pursuit of change. Effective leadership is really about turning intangibles to tangibles that can be appreciated by many beneficiaries.

- **Effective communication**: The best-defined goals are not achievable if they are not effectively communicated. A leader selects a range of multi-purpose communication styles to deliver the message. He must be seen to be non-partisan in attitude and communicate candidly in every situation. Closely associated with this quality is the flair for networking and coordinating among diverse personalities. Some communities are more advanced than others in their openness to communication. This demands a multifaceted approach using various methods that have proved effective in the circumstances. It would be foolhardy to use print media for disseminating crucial matters through a community where illiteracy is predominant. Perhaps verbal consultation is more suitable in that situation. Thus a good leader understands these nuances.

- **Organisational excellence:** Good leadership entails astute planning of tactics and processes of dealing with perceived problems. The uniqueness of leadership is the ability to make that extra effort to see what the populace cannot easily see and put it into a problem-solving structure.

  I recall as a child how my father and a friend mobilised a small rural community to build a primary school. This was a pioneering farming community. There were no roads or developed infrastructure of any form. These two men mobilised the community to prioritise their needs. Building a school was top of the list. The community made its own bricks, cut grass for thatching, cut poles from the forest and built the first two classrooms. Aware that the government of the day was not keen to educate blacks, the leaders approached an evangelical missionary group to give financial support for books and teachers. This venture was so successful that a prominent school *was born which has since produced many eminent citizens. Incidentally, I was among its first products and have since contributed much to its upgrading. On a larger scale there are many self-help schemes across Africa such as Masakhane in South Africa, Ujamaa in Tanzania, Mushandir-apamwe in Zimbabwe. These are products of excellent leaders who convinced the masses of their worthiness.*

- **Selective non-conformism:** *Effective community leaders should adhere to professional management art and science but should sometimes be maverick in their behaviour. Unpredictable non-conformity can be an effective vanguard for effecting change in society. On our continent there are ample success stories of trade union leaders becoming political and community stalwarts for change. This meant breaking out of the mould of legislative dictates to take an unexpected stance. By so doing, many of the leaders risked their freedom and lives in pursuit of change and in most cases won the battle. Conformity is predictable and boring to the extent of arousing cynicism sometimes, instead of mobilising community support. But non-conformism does not mean ultra vires action which disregards the basic laws of humanity. Instead it means observing the rule of law as regards the fundamentals of society but highlighting the incongruencies which affect that community with respect to selected issues. So it follows that criminals and law-breakers cannot be community leaders. Non-conformity means electing to handle an ordinary situation differently for optimal results under different circumstances.*

- **Lateral thinking:** *This trait is akin to non-conformism except that it does not imply doing the unexpected. Instead, it refers to an active cognitive process that scans the environment for cues for solutions to problems. An effective leader must consider all the ramifications to a situation in searching for the right way to handle it. This implies challenging the status quo to see things in a different light and perceive the obvious before others do. If this is done well, that person attains such authority (respect due to expertise) that community members defer to him or her for solutions to serious problems. A*

107

lateral thinker is often a visionary and innovator who acts as the torchbearer for followers. Thus one-track-minded bigots who propound the same doctrine year in year out are not real community leaders.

- **Dramatic moves:** Good leadership also calls for the ability to make dramatic moves with speed. Speed refers to decision making, selecting appropriate courses of action and choosing lieutenants to assist with the community work. The first action is to discuss the problems to deepen understanding and facilitate consensual action. Once that general predisposition has beens created the leader should take over and act swiftly. It is unrealistic to expect total agreement to every situation, hence the virtue of the principle of consensus which ignores the few dissenting voices. It is more honourable for a leader to be accused of making a hasty decision rather than not making a decision at all.

- **Positive aggressiveness for success:** There is an age-old debate on whether leaders are born or made. Certainly leadership calls for a personality structure different from the ordinary. Much of this can be the result of conscious or subliminal learning from role models (living or dead) and the environment. The fuel that propels a good leader to success is consistent aggressiveness, which becomes the self-fulfilling prophecy of 'The harder I work, the more successful I become'.

  The road to success is strewn with thorns – particularly when unpopular decisions have to be made which isolate the leader from sycophants. At that stage only the internally generated need for achievement remains the fuel for success. This brings to the fore another vital component of this quality which relates to the paradox of popularity and leadership. A good leader does not always score 100% in popularity polls. The sheer nature of leadership decisions breeds unpopularity. However, as long as the decision is based on factual grounds, and passes the four-way test of truth, correctness, rightness and helpfulness, a leader should press on without regard to popularity. Thus, a leader must have the guts to succeed.

Strategic visionary: *Effective leadership requires a strategic match between hindsight and foresight. Without being ruled by precedent, it is vital to know the cause-effect relationship of previous events and use the knowledge to minimise the margin of error in future predictions. This is the ethos of scenario planning. The subtle difference between leaders and the led is that leaders see solutions and opportunities which others miss. Strategic visionaries blend human strengths and opportunities to eliminate weaknesses and achieve communal goals to the satisfaction of all concerned. That is the contribution of visionary leadership to customer service in the community context.*

Over the last decade I have observed with admiration a top trade unionist in the national labour movement of Zimbabwe. The country has slid into economic desperation due to bad political leadership at national, provincial and community levels, leading to harsh living conditions for the ordinary person. The worker's movement has become the only formidable agency for change. Consequently, this trade unionist has led millions of workers into real resistance against corruption and abuse of power. He has maintained clear focus of who his customers are and what mandate they gave him. He is aware of his career anchor lying not in politics but in labour issues.

COMMUNITY WITH NO LEADERSHIP?

Perhaps the logical question is whether it is necessary to have community leaders, considering the mammoth problems they sometimes bring entailing nepotism, corruption, greed and lack of performance. Fortunately the answer seems to be in the affirmative. Leaders accomplish more good than the bad attributed to them. Even in a near-classless society like Switzerland there are discernible leadership structures which serve as the glue that sticks communities together.

Communities are the building blocks which make up the whole society. Ideally the structure should be so well synchronised that community leaders should sit at the top of the pyramid as a management team creating an enabling environment for all the community members to have their needs met with respect to transport, security, social activities, sport, civic administration and education. Like typical customers, the populace should have direct and easy access to the leaders as providers of service, to complain against poor service or absence of it. Good community leadership gives a constructive and accommodating character to society as a whole.

An example is Uganda in East Africa, which slid into lawlessness as a result of political dictatorship in the 1970s. The new democratic leadership has since made marvellous achievements in restoring the rule of law and human dignity. Today community leadership structures exist where villagers and city dwellers elect their own leaders responsible for security, development, health, education and so forth. The results have been remarkable with crime declining to negligible levels. These communities have succeeded because of good leadership. The great challenge is to instil meaningful leadership skills across the community in the family, church, school, workplace and public arena. Such inculcation must impart the virtues of honesty, management integrity and rule of law, and define the superordinate goal which transcends ethnic and colour lines. Community leadership does not have to be politically correct all the time. Political leadership customers must be viewed differently from community level customers. Often the two are erroneously interchanged, and service standards suffer.

COMPREHENSIVE SOCIETAL REORIENTATION

An integral part of handling the affairs of the public is an underlying set of principles such as transparency, public accountability, hierarchy and participative leadership. It means the whole community should have a common perception of right and wrong as well as a service standards benchmark. Significant and long-term commitment to quality service requires a comprehensive approach built on a new understanding of the world around it. Here are some of the principles.

OWNERSHIP

Whenever a community improvement programme is introduced in a locality, there ought to be the full conviction that it is owned by all the inhabitants. If there is an impression that the programme or project has been imposed on the community by leaders or external agents the likelihood of it being sabotaged or boycotted is high. Many examples can be cited from all over Africa during the colonial period and, sadly, even afterwards in some isolated cases. In rural areas provincial or district development councils were responsible for the construction of essential infrastructure such as roads, dip tanks for cattle, business growth points, bridges, community halls and schools. On the surface they were self-governing entities which set their priorities for which funds were allocated by central government for development. In practice the provincial commissioner and district commissioner were the ultimate adjudicators over the disbursement of funds. Instead of consulting the grassroots community members on their desired priority projects, tailored within the available funds, they decided for them. Worse still, the doctrine of separate development of different racial groups was prevalent in most countries which led to more funds being channelled towards the white communities while blacks were left impoverished and encouraged to mount self-help projects for fund raising.

The social consequences of this lack of ownership by the respective communities were drastic. In periods of political or community uprisings the first targets for destruction were cattle dip tanks, bridges and similar structures that the community clearly saw as belonging to the government and not to themselves. In the cities community halls, market places and schools were frequently targeted for the same reasons.

BUSINESS-LINKED

Communities are crucial parts of the cosmos of society, and their prosperity is dependent on the general growth of business enterprise in that society.

In Africa development is concentrated in isolated towns and cities, which results in major rural to urban migration in search of improved social facilities. That migration puts unbearable pressure on the limited social services in the cities, causing them to become mediocre services which do not satisfy their original customers.

Many communities are good at generating life skills for growing food and providing the basics of life. However, these village economies do not lead to sustained prosperity if they are not linked to external, more progressive, business activities. An ideal community development model should be one where each demarcated small society exports from its area the products most needed elsewhere and buys from outside what it requires. This miniature balance of payments would ensure equal development of social services for the various communities making up one nation.

LEADERSHIP

Human beings are inherently amenable to leadership. In a family they are subjected to parental leadership. At school they are subjected to the teachers' leadership, which instils the values of life. For the rest of their lives people have to yield at different times to different forces of leadership, such as an employer or work superior, civic and business organisation leaders and political leaders.

This analogy goes some way towards proving that leadership is the driving force that determines the direction and pace of community growth. In some countries in our region central government services have been successfully developed down to small communities, to the extent that each village has a health worker trained to dispense minor, common treatment, and a judicial committee which hears small cases of community disagreements and refers to the magistrates' court what it cannot resolve. These activities and many other developmental efforts are coordinated by a chairperson or committee. These leaders must be fully trained to be able to steer the community and keep pace with developments in the outer society.

Service orientation is the critical quality in key players in this community service network. Volunteer or elected officials have taken it upon themselves to serve others. In most of these communities poverty is pronounced and only subsistence farming sustains them. Compare the service spirit of a villager who is called while hoeing his crops by someone who wants some medicine from the village medicine chest to a qualified nurse in an established hospital. The villager is sacrificing earning his living in the fields yet he does it gladly, while the professional nurse sometimes sulks and complains of being overworked. Who is the real service hero? Undoubtedly the villager who incurs considerable opportunity cost and yet loves serving others. These are the frontliners who make a difference in society. That is service excellence in the community setting.

COMMUNITY MANAGEMENT

The task of leading community effort must be viewed in the same light as business management. Indeed it is as crucial, for it impacts on hundreds of lives, apart from the absence of the profit motive. In private business 85% of what happens is attributable to the management. The same equation should apply without pre-qualification to the community setting. To this end it is necessary for those playing a management role to be given the tools and training to establish the guiding service quality criteria.

TOTAL QUALITY

Any community service effort must involve everybody with the understanding that quality is not optional but is part of everybody's responsibility. It must not be left to uninterested individuals who wish to pursue their own interests. The pursuit of quality must link the present minds of the community to the future challenges, building on present strengths.

It must promote the philosophy of continuous improvement, considering that the journey to excellence is a journey, not a destination. Therefore, the need is for a sustained, structured programme that is managed and developed as a central part of community activities. Quality service orientation must lead to the development of service standards for every part of the community, recognising that quality for the external customer must be built on quality service between individuals and groups within the community and standards must be visible at all times.

REWARD FOR DELIVERY

Communities must mete out sanctions and reward quality delivery where evidence exists. An old adage goes thus: 'What gets measured and what gets rewarded is what gets done.' For the most part, community leadership, like many public positions, is a thankless job. It invites more criticism than praise. However, reward can be given to excellent community leadership through public accolade or re-election to the same or higher office. While I believe that local community structures should remain apolitical, I see merit in community leaders being elected as a reward for good performance to higher national political leadership posts. After all, they have proven themselves in public accountability and transparency.

Chapter 7

The African service Renaissance

There is a tide in the affairs of men
Which, taken at the flood, leads on to fortune.
Omitted, all the voyage of their life
Is bound in shallows and in miseries

On such a full sea are we now afloat,
And we must take the current when it serves,
Or lose our ventures.

(Shakespeare, Julius Caesar)

These words were uttered by Cassius while urging his compatriots to proceed with the plot to murder Julius Caesar and they were sufficiently powerful to motivate them to accomplish their mission. The wisdom of the Shakespearean era is also symbolic of contemporary African society. For, in the order of wealth of nations, most of the countries on our continent have hit the bottom of the poverty pit and are now either levelling out or emerging from the abyss.

African Renaissance is the vanguard of change currently sweeping across the continent as a new dawn to prime up cooperation and self-reliance essential for socio-economic development. As a way of giving new order to society it carries the potential of becoming more dominant than the wave of pan-Africanism which prevailed from the 1950s. This philosophy is being driven by fairly young political leaders such as presidents Thabo Mbeki of South Africa, Yoweri Museveni of Uganda, Jerry Rawlings of Ghana and Joachim Chissano of Mozambique. In addition, the world's political and economic order is moving towards regional blocs with an all-inclusive developmental agenda. As a vehicle for changing the orientation as well as the renewal of African society, the concept of renaissance probably stands the best chance of all. More so, it is seen as an apolitical, purely developmental economic integration to serve hundreds of millions of customers in the region. The existence of such demarcations as the Southern African Development Community (SADC), the Preferrential Trade Area (PTA), the Economic Organisation of West African states (Ecowas) and the East African Community Trading Bloc should provide a solid foundation for African Renaissance.

THE RUBBER MEETS THE ROAD

To the African continent reality is becoming increasingly challenging as some of the Western countries shift their stance from supportive to sceptical. There are no more automatic financial handouts, and they now seek some quid pro quo instead. A similarly coordinated reaction is apparent from the International Monetary Fund, the World Bank, the Paris Club and others.

Another challenge arises from the more critical internal expectations of our society today. These range from good governance and improved quality of life to a progressive economy with its resultant benefits. A few decades ago it was rare to stage demonstrations about social issues against a democratically elected government. Today it is common practice in most of our cities.

Further challenges arise from the onslaught of the virtual village because of the technological explosion. The arrival of Internet and the information superhighway has shrunk the world to a common market of homogeneous needs. Local providers of seemingly basic services now face competition from challengers from USA and Europe. The deciding factor is no longer just who produces the best product, but who follows up with more effective, personal and value-added services. For many direct consumer goods such as electrical appliances, educational material, do-it-yourself domestic items and even basic medical supplies one can order on the Internet from any destination in the world within seconds and receive them within 24 hours. A case in point is AMWAY (that is, American Way) which is a mail order supplier of a comprehensive range of household supplies. It has taken Africa by storm and poses serious competition to local suppliers and retailers through local distribution centres. The delivery turnaround time can be faster than a local merchant who is not geared to meet prompt requests for service. The time has come for the apathetic 'fat cats' in business to either make a total change to be highly responsive to market needs or inevitably be driven out of business. The forces of global competition are too mighty to resist and they carry no passengers.

Another reality is that production-driven economic growth has been superceded by service-oriented growth. There is a discernible shift from high-industry smoke-stack economy to high-knowledge service economy. Therefore, the critical success factor is no longer how you make a commodity but whether you produce what the customers want, make it available when, where and in the form in which they want it. Again the aftercare service resulting from product beneficiation is vital. Brand building and its sustenance are now easy because of the constant information flow across continents. Such brands as Coca Cola, McDonald's, Microsoft, Boeing, Levi Jeans, Sony and Samsung bear testimony to this foreign challenge.

Even more acute challenges emanate from a more critical African society than ever before. It is now open to internal competitiveness because of increased education. Easy and ready accessibility to the external world has brought more open-mindedness with increased capacity for imitation leading to less originality of choice. If one walks through some of the downtown streets of African cities, one might momentarily believe that one was in New York or London because of the clothes and behavioural trends.

Another distinct set of challenges are posed by the inevitability of change. A basic rule of survival now demands a predominance of innovation for improvement. The principle of incremental changes

(Japanese *Kaizen*) becomes a reality for meaningful change to occur. Second, the human race is fast becoming obsessed with electronics and IT. Think of the quantum leap electronic banking has brought to customer service in the financial services industry. Third, there will be high human mobility and less rigidity of boundaries. SADC is actively considering a common regional labour market and free trade. The East African community has made greater advances in that regard, while the Southern African Customs Union (SACU) established a common trading and monetary area a long time ago. This is bound to give rise to a more discerning mass market with some real demands on customer service. Such a large market will inevitably create a beneficial critical mass due to economies of scale, which cannot accrue to localised small markets.

CONTINUING MOMENTS OF TRUTH

Once again we revisit the phenomenon of the split seconds in which service providers interact with their customers and create first impressions. In the private sector customers will seek to judge whether the product or service is a rip-off or is beneficial to them. By the same token, political customers will want to draw a dividing line between exploitation and enriching experience. Any trace of exploitation often leads to a public outcry to embarrass the leaders and seek redress. In the public and parastatal environment attention will be focused on whether the organisation is corruption-ridden or an efficient service machinery. Professions will be judged on their capacity to add value to the service expected by their clients rather than pursue purely commercial self-enrichment. Not least, community-based service providers will be scrutinised to see if they adopt an altruistic dedication to grass-roots development or are bound in myopic individualism. The acid test is this question: 'Are we planting the seed today for tomorrow's growth or engaged in terminal short-term efforts?'

To show that bad service is a function of the human element and that neither Africa nor Europe is exempt from it, I will share with you two parallel true stories, which happened to two of my close family friends. Both incidents lie squarely in the medical profession across the two continents. The first story is about a lady friend who lived in Switzerland for four years with her husband and children in the early 1990s. She fell ill and was admitted to hospital where she was first diagnosed of one thing and then another, both of which turned out to be wrong. In the third week the illness was correctly diagnosed and she was operated upon without any real emotional preparation. The family were informed it would be a minor operation from which she would recover within a couple of days. In reality she languished in hospital for a further month because the operation had been done wrongly, giving rise to life-threatening complications. Immediately after being discharged, she flew back home, where doctors condemned the manner in which she was operated, indicating she had a prima facie case for suing the hospital for negligence. She now has a large unsightly permanent scar. No apology was extended and she vowed that she will never be treated in a European hospital again.

Another couple lived in South Africa while on an expatriate posting with an international firm. The wife went into maternity hospital to deliver her first child. An operation was performed which turned out to be unsuccessful because the abdominal cut would not heal. Instead of being out of hospital in three days, this became two weeks of agony. In the meantime, the nurse who was supposed to feed the infant did not do it, whilst the mother could not walk to go to the room where the baby was. Consequently, her husband had to come twice a day, including 01h00 in the morning, to feed his child. When he asked the nurse why she was not doing her duty, she retorted that was not part of her job. One could ask a barrage of questions such as: If tending the sick is not a nurse's job then what are they trained and employed to do? Couldn't sheer human compassion persuade her to help the woman in pain? While a nurse set her own rules, where were the supervisors? Is there a shared vision and purpose for existence in this hospital?

In each case something technically wrong was done, but no one took the responsibility either to redress it or to apologise. This is a breach of the first cardinal rule of service excellence. Second, in neither case did the institution display an inherent culture of service orientation. Consequently, the staff were only doing a job to earn their salary with no passion for service. This breaches another cardinal rule, which advocates love for what one does. Third, each incident was a catastrophic moment of truth that influenced the attitude of each family negatively. Each family will recount the nightmare for years, thereby spreading a negative image of the country in general and the medical profession in particular. Thousands of highly professional and caring staff are being painted with the one negative brush.

BEYOND RENAISSANCE TO WORLD CLASS

There is no panacea but only a practical recipe for success in such circumstances as Africa finds itself. Let us enumerate the ten service commandments and put them into a framework of logic, which can assist those in search of excellence.

- **First:** *Build on the virtues of our Africanness, which were detailed in the first chapter, that is, the inherent unpretentious originality, warmth, communal helpfulness and genuineness. The Japanese emerged from the ashes of World War II into a world-class economic Goliath by building on their work ethic. For decades Western productivity gurus flocked to Japan to study their rise. It was that dedicated employment-for-life ethic that enabled the transformation of Tokyo Tsushin Kogyo from a relatively small company to the world giant called Sony today. Many others followed suit, adding to considerable customer satisfaction across the universe.*

- **Two:** Service standards are notably elevated in an environment where the spirit of nationhood and little or no ethnocentrism prevails. Tribal delineations and racial disharmony militate against service excellence as they prevent maximum tapping of the best talent in society. The fact that someone is related to you, comes from your neighbourhood, or is of the same racial origin does not make him or her the best performer in a position you may have at your disposal. In most African contexts the biggest scourges are nepotism, villagism, sexism, parochialism and aversion to diversity of approach. These are all arch-enemies of service excellence.

- **Three:** Adopting an international frame of reference for self-appraisal as opposed to accepting a second-best sub-optimal position. A dull student who comes first in a class of sub-standard peers does not become a genius. The human mind and society have a natural self-defence mechanism whereby when unsuccessful they look for a scapegoat by comparing themselves with one of lesser capability. We should benchmark ourselves against the best and not say: 'We are just Africans.' Some of the best holiday resorts in Africa are those where the local culture is totally entrenched in the service without any Western or foreign frills, where you are received in an African manner, into a place livened with African décor, entertained and fed in a typically African fashion. How should service excellence be measured under such circumstances? Only one way prevails – by the customers exclaiming: 'Wow, I never expected that.' Africans earn this every day, but the trumpet is not blown loud enough by those who judge collective performance.

- **Four:** Distinctive competence: What is it that we clearly excel in? Comparative advantage: What are we better endowed with than others? Africa has much to show in this regard. In the area of people, we have peace-loving, hardworking, enduring and emotionally rich people. For this reason they make excellent tour guides. In terms of natural resources we are to be envied by the world. Begin with our vast open sparsely populated land, rich vegetation and thick forests, the huge game reserves well stocked with animals, the picturesque terrain, including world landmarks such as Mount Kilimanjaro, the Zambezi with Victoria Falls, the East African Great Lakes, and the Sahara desert.

All these features are great selling points for service experience for foreigners. It is our in-born hospitality that enables our visitors to experience the African jungles by night and day without fearing for their lives. That is a combination of distinctive competence and comparative advantage.

- **Five:** Our society should build on its propensity to consensus and team spirit to become a continually learning society. We need a value-adding education system which sharpens life skills more than solving abstract problems of the universe. A learning society believes in multi-directional change and discards precedent as the sole yardstick for right and wrong. Similarly, it seeks to benchmark its performance against the best and not the mediocre. More so, it has a shared vision and promotes team learning. Africans can score highly because they have the requisite emotional interdependence and sentimental identification with what is perceived as the intangible but omniscient and omnipotent force responsible for societal discipline and wisdom.

- **Six:** Political stability and peace: any form of service can only be dispensed in conditions of relative calmness. This makes stability of society a prerequisite for service excellence. An equally vital condition is less governance, which gives people the leeway for creativity and personal responsibility for own actions. The only fly in the African ointment is instability as evidenced by civil wars and autocratic governments. These give rise to a state of mental emergency that militates against customer care of any form.

- **Seven:** African culture must strike the delicate balance between communalism and positive individual competition. To be world class an inherent spirit of competitiveness must be embraced by all. Sadly, a rare concept of 'PhD' prevails among those frustrated by the stiff competition brought about by the present-day cut-throat conditions. That acronym does not stand for an academic doctorate degree at all. It means simply 'Pull him *or her down', which refers to frustrating the efforts of any colleague who appears to be exceeding the norm for success. That is reminiscent of communalism translated lock, stock and barrel from the traditional agrarian setting to the modern cash economy. Consequently, it militates against service excellence.*

- **Eight:** *Total quality commitment: service excellence is a direct corollary of the quality philosophy. Society and its constituent groups must have an extremely high work ethic and self-discipline, which will make it forego something of interest to ensure excellent service to others. Quality is an elusive phenomenon that is only recognised by recipients and compels them to repeatedly buy that service and not one offered by a competitor. We have seen how Japanese society rose to fame through their relentless quality-dominated work ethic. The African is the most resilient person to hard conditions, which breeds an extremely hard-working nature. The virtues of that high work ethic can be mobilised into a laudable quality-oriented service vehicle that will win us a place in the sun.*

- **Nine:** *Big and audacious societal goals. American society built its success around the 'American dream', which promises every member of society a high quality of life. This became a distinctive ethos that instilled the value system of a winning nation. That has been the rallying point for centuries, making it the world economic powerhouse. There are striking geopolitical similarities between the United States and Africa. The USA is a union of 51 states and Africa has a similar number of countries. That is why Kwame Nkrumah saw it was possible to create the United States of Africa as early as the 1960s. The fundamental difference lies in gross national wealth and per capita income. However, we have the necessary ingredients to transform into a winning continent. What will it take? Only a highly potent formula of ambition and determination to rise from the trenches of deprivation. There is an old African adage which says 'There is dignity in poverty' that seeks to show that it is always possible to turn around from poverty to dignity. We can do it.*

Big, hairy, audacious goals (Bhags) stimulate progress by stretching the ability and capacity of people. The fact that one dares to tread where the devils fear makes one a visionary who sets compelling goals for oneself and others. Such tough and unimaginable goals have a clear finishing line. In addition, they serve as highly motivating. It's exciting to fight against Goliath and it's even more exciting to beat him. These big goals should transcend leadership and promote entrepreneurship. In so doing, the pursuit for Bhags reinforces the core ideology.

- **Ten:** *From time telling to clock building. Quality and service demand that providers stay ahead of the game to retain a competitive age. This requires a mindset of innovation and adventurousness. A time-telling society follows changes with no influence on the course of things. It watches things happen and sometimes wonders what happened. On the other hand, a clock-building society invests energy in building sustainable structures and processes to deliver excellence in the desired form. African society has already demonstrated its capacity to build clocks and help others to tell the correct time through the wonders of such monuments as the Egyptian pyramids, Great Zimbabwe, bushmen caves and paintings all over the continent which represented landmarks of historical progress. That competitive strategy can only grow from strength to strength.*

  Society must value change experimentation and constant improvement. It is necessary to make a shift in thinking as fundamental as that which preceded the Newtonian revolution. Prior to that revolution, people explained the world around them primarily in terms of a God that made specific decisions. This theory of causality is the basis of explanation of events in all ordinary African situations. In the 1600s people figured out that God put in place a universe with certain principles, relieving God of the burden of making all minute decisions. From then on people learned to look for the underlying dynamics of the universal system which caused things to happen as they do. That was the essence of the Newtonian revolution. This self-sustaining set of principles is the sole evidence of being in the clock-building mode.

QUEST FOR AFRICAN SERVICE RENEWAL

We have been at pains to describe the magnanimous nature of African leaders who sacrificed everything to gain freedom for the masses. This was captured so lucidly by Thabo Mbeki, who is today president of South Africa. In 1964, as a young man, he addressed the United Nations Special Committee Against Apartheid in London. He was echoing the voice of black Africans against persecution in general and appealing for the lives of those politicians found guilty of treason at the Rivonia trial in Johannesburg, among whom were his father and Nelson Mandela. Undeterred he spoke forcefully saying:

> *Though much has been said on this subject, I should also like to add my testimony about the character of the men that the South African government would have the world believe are criminals. They are not only men of the greatest integrity that responsibility to their families and friends would demand, men who would be welcomed by any civilised country, but also men who would grace any government in which they served. Activated by the noblest of motives, they have acquired through the years an understanding of leadership that would be a valuable contribution to the common human experience ... Today we might be but weak children, spurred on by nothing other than the fear and grief of losing our fathers. In time yet we shall learn to die both for ourselves and for the millions.*

Undoubtedly this was the epitome of selfless service by leaders who were prepared to lay down their lives for the freedom of the masses. Today it would not be surprising to hear anyone who is told of this sacrifice exclaiming 'Wow, I did not expect them to do that.' That statement is synonymous with service excellence. A handful of people created a vision in the interest of the rest of the society and pursued it with passion. After the 1994 democratic elections in South Africa, Thabo Mbeki became the architect and chief protagonist of the quest for African Renaissance. To this end he made very strong assertions in 1998:

> The time has come that we say enough and no more, and by acting to banish the shame remake ourselves as the midwives of the African Renaissance. An ill wind has blown me across the face of Africa. I have seen the poverty of Orlando East and the wealth of Morningside in Johannesburg. In Lusaka, I have seen the poor Kanyama township and the prosperous residence of Kabulonga. I have seen the African slums of Surulere in Lagos and the African opulence of Victoria Island. I have seen the faces of the poor in Mbare in Harare and the quiet wealth of Borrowdale. I have had the stories of how those who had access to power, or access to those who had access to power, of how they have robbed and pillaged and broken all laws and all ethical norms with great abandon to acquire wealth, all of them tied by an invisible thread which they hope would connect them to Morningside and Borrowdale and Victoria Island and Kabulonga ...
>
> It is out of this pungent mixture of greed, dehumanising poverty, obscene wealth and endemic public and private corrupt practice that many of Africa's coups d'etat, civil wars and situations of instability are born and entrenched ...
>
> The African Renaissance demands that we purge ourselves of the parasites and maintain a permanent vigilance against the danger of the entrenchment in African society of the rapacious stratum with its social morality according to which everything in society must be organised materially to benefit the few ...
>
> Surely, there must be politicians and women activists, trade unionists, religious leaders, artists and professionals from Cape to Cairo, from Madagascar to Cape Verde, who are sufficiently enraged by Africa's condition in the world to want to join the mass crusade for Africa's renewal.

It is heartening to listen to such a prominent African leader advocating for a new service platform for Africans to define their own agenda to deliver service excellence across their continent. Future prosperity rests on the success of such ideologies being translated to common daily practice by the common person. Indeed Africa still has ample opportunity for a turnaround.

PULLING THE THREADS TOGETHER

The simple service excellence equation is as follows.

At any given time in a business transaction the level of actual service is greater than or equal to the perception of the recipient. It means the service provided must equal or exceed the perception of the recipient of the service. Business is all about people and not rocket science. It is about people as customers or consumers of services and products. It is also about people as staff and management creating and providing the service. Lastly, it is about people as suppliers of the hardware and raw material to craft the service or product to be given. Therefore, a fundamental principle of service excellence is to eliminate dissonance by promoting a common perception and vision of service among all three categories of people involved in the business transaction.

Close the service gap in every walk of life. This can be achieved through all sectors of organised society including private and public sectors, the political sphere and the professions committing themselves to the following steps:

- *Providing management training for deeper perception and open-mindedness in understanding situations*
- *Creating an environment conducive to service excellence through teamwork and quality-oriented productivity*
- *Empowering all staff through a supportive management style, a less structured climate and training to boost their service skills*

127

- *Instituting in-built self-audits for organisations to facilitate evaluation of their performance in regard to service provision.*

Encourage hypermetropia (long-sightedness) in all concerned with the distribution chain. Service providers need to have clearer knowledge of the outer world to fend off xenophobia. They should be able to see further than their noses in order to use objective benchmarks for comparison. They should have the courage to unravel tradition, break the mould and redefine the norms of service. Precedent must not be allowed to supplant new moves towards customer-oriented behaviour.

Chapter 8

Crystal ball into the new millennium

In conclusion let us discuss the relationship between service excellence and the mobilisation of a new African society to meet global competitiveness. This entails constructing a thumbnail sketch of the new beginning for this beloved continent. Let us attune our minds through the inspiring words of Theodore Roosevelt, president of the United States of America as far back as 1899. 'Far better to dare mighty things, to win glorious triumphs, even though checkered by failure, than to take rank with those poor spirits who neither enjoy much nor suffer much because they live in the grey twilight that knows not victory nor defeat!' These words exalt the virtues of embarking on big audacious goals whether as an individual or as a nation. Therefore, it requires significant changing in African society at various levels.

TWENTY-FIRST CENTURY AFRICAN SOCIETY

To achieve the noble but elusive objectives of the African economic revival, the society must undergo wholesale transformation.

The most fundamental society upheaval will be in its value system. The future generation will have a higher level of self-esteem, which will motivate it to reach for much higher goals than those of the past. Such conjecture flows from the current thinking that the last century discovered human dignity of the underprivileged of the world and the twenty-first century will assert the place of the African in the determination of world affairs. To illustrate this elevation of the value system, a common model of human behavioural motivation will be discussed in relation to our society, namely Maslow's hierarchical theory of motivation. It sought to explain why people are driven by particular needs at certain times, which leads to them valuing internally driven needs. A society is ruled by its value system, which implies that perception or experiencing of customer service satisfaction is largely determined by one's value system. Maslow's theory propagates that an individual, and collectively a society, has an ascending order of needs which primarily influence his or her behaviour. The ripple effect goes on until the highest level need is satisfied.

Graphically the pyramid of needs is represented in this form.

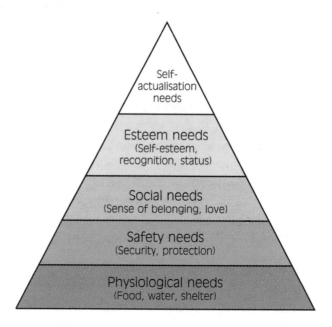

The simple interpretation of the five categories of needs is that when a person feels hungry or thirsty or needs shelter from inclement weather, he or she is preoccupied with satisfying that need. At that time the person is not concerned with such higher order needs as personal safety, or being loved or attaining a recognised status in the community or, finally, realising his or her highest potential in life. Only when the person's hunger is eliminated does he or she worry about personal safety and the pattern is repeated through all the need categories.

Let us now relate this to our contemporary African society. The overwhelming majority of indigenous African inhabitants are at the physiological and safety needs level on the Maslow hierarchy. This is because of several factors, including the widespread poverty brought about by lack of economic advancement, rampant wars, civil unrest and social displacement, famine caused by poor agrarian practices, as well as lack of farming implements. Consequently, most of our societies have chasms between a small elite and masses of poverty-stricken compatriots. Naturally this impacts seriously on the concept and practice of service excellence.

First, the majority living in poverty automatically become subservient to the small elite for survival. The elite internalise the tendency to exploit the defenceless masses because they have little or no bargaining power to demand decent levels of service. With time, bad service, including exploitation, becomes more of the rule than the exception. Eventually the entire society is maligned by this self-perpetuating evil.

Second, the small elite fail to see the need to comply with any decent norms of service because they define the rules and shift the goalposts as they deems beneficial to their interests. In this regard we often experience unethical business practices, exorbitant pricing structures and lack of sensitivity to market demands.

Third, in response to this apparent exploitation the poor masses tend to become persuaded to abrogate the rule of law and start by perpetrating petty crime to feed themselves. If this goes unchecked by redistribution of wealth or other social equity measures, society degenerates into anarchy. Thus, poor or lack of service excellence begets lawlessness if it is ignored for too long. There is an old axiom which says, 'The rich cannot sleep well at night if their neighbour is starving'.

Even more serious are the social and psychological consequences of constantly struggling to satisfy the first two levels of basic needs on the Maslow hierarchy. The core of the self-esteem and pride of the nation is hurt, forcing it into mediocre low achievement mode. Underachievers can never become winners, whether as individuals or as collective society. The corollary is that losers do not serve well in any circumstances. The hypothesis is that twenty-first century society in African countries will be emancipated from economic deprivation, which in turn will enable it to satisfy social needs, then proceed to meet the self-esteem and finally the self-actualisation needs. Society will create and uphold a new value system driven by service excellence as the normal way of doing business. In short, tomorrow's African society will have a higher motivational level than its brow-beaten forerunners of today.

POLITICAL LANDSCAPE

The logical point of departure is to ask a myriad of questions about African politics:

- *Is there going to be another Rwanda 1994 genocide anywhere else on the continent?*
- *Will political intolerance of rival political parties continue to be the hallmark of African politics?*
- *Will tribalism and ethnic orientation continue to dictate political conduct in African nations?*
- *Can racial exclusiveness defy the laws of nature and prevent total integration of races?*
- *Does open democracy have a chance in the African political scenario or will a modified version dominate the future?*
- *Will the rivalry among African nations give way to continentalism to face the world as a formidable alliance?*
- *Is there going to be a preference for peace in the Horn of Africa, North Africa, West Africa, the Equatorial Belt, East and Southern Africa?*
- *Is there going to be a successful, humane solution to the problem of 6 million refugees currently on our continent?*

These are daunting questions which should be uppermost in the minds of all Africans. The answers have a great deal of effect on service and the environment of delivery to the many citizens who expect continuous improvement in their lives. Here are my predictions for the African political scenario, and its impact on the millions of its customers.

First, an effect of the winds of change will be erosion of close-knit ethnical constellations in favour of mass national democracies. This will mean that all over the continent marginalised groups such as the coloureds and those of Indian origin will take their place squarely alongside indigenous Africans or, euphemistically, very black Africans. This will have far-reaching positive spin-offs as regards wealth creation and building the economy when these groupings completely feel that they are part of the African dynasty who must play their part in the renaissance and reconstruction process.

Second, an obvious direct result of the above developments will be the creation of a more acute sense of nationhood. Politics of exclusion were fashionable in the century just ended when national profiles were still overtly checkered with tribal, ethnic and racial polarisation. These will be of no major consequence in the new century because of a natural process of evolution of mankind, wisdom as well as political maturation dictated by new reality.

When I and all the black Africans of my generation and before grew up, separate development between races was the norm. As a result, each side of the colour line internalised the false reality that the other side was of no importance, except where it served an economic purpose as an employer or employee. As opportunities opened up because of political overhauls, this became a fallacy. In addition, social integration through housing, schooling, sharing of social amenities and business equality have enforced a new order. When I went to school, my only option was a black-only school and I only met other races at university. Ten years later my child attended a multi-racial kindergarten and school from day one. The definition of racism that I carry is totally different from the perception that she and her contemporaries of other races have. Theirs is a level playing field that promotes the commonality of nationhood. To that effect, when they define standards of service, they do so through the same viewpoint to similar audience.

The third ingredient of a healthy political landscape will be professional leadership on the part of those entrusted with the affairs of the nation. The politics of yesteryear were symbolised by lack of service mentality, blatant exploitation of opponents, intolerance of opposite views and absence of transparency or accountability to those being served. Ethical behaviour was encountered more by accident than by design in most leadership. They should not be entirely blamed for they were responding to an environment which promoted such behaviour. To this day many political leaders are using their powerbase to advance business opportunities for themselves and their kindred.

Such crossovers tend to lead to conflict of interests, anti-trust and sometimes downright corruption. These slip-ups do not go unnoticed by the rank and file, who adopt them as the new mode of survival. The politician of the new century will either be young and well-off or old, mature and affluent from years of hard work. The two ends of the spectrum will be preferred because they will have the best chance of being content with politics alone and not cross over to the private business arena simultaneously.

Professional leadership skills will be the order of the day to be able to create and foster a vision, correctly decipher the political nuances at play, employ the correct decision logic despite insufficient information and be completely results-oriented. Thus, in the new century, political office will become an elected sign of achievement instead of being the dumping ground for mediocre party stalwarts. African politics will become more internationally oriented both for individual nations and for the consolidated continent. Africa will have to claim its rightful position as an international player and not remain in the second league of nations. This will be achieved mainly through three strategies. One will depend on our capability to curb civil wars, unrests and factional rivalry. The second is dependent on demonstrated preference for peace across the continent. Intra-continental organisations such as OAU, SADC, ECOWAS, the Arabic African Countries League, PTA, East African Countries bloc will have to consistently sell the message of peace preference. Political players of the future will have the humility of servant leadership and thus will identify with their constituents as customers for life.

The third factor is the extent of economic progress to make Africa a force to be reckoned with on the global map. If African economies boom sufficiently to be able to feed their people, employ their economically active populations, provide adequate social security facilities and do not depend on borrowing from the IMF-World Bank Consortium, the world will look at Africa as a serious contributor to universal progress and not a millstone retarding international prosperity. This will require an incisively new look at the relationship of politics and business by political leaders of the future.

The new century will see an Africa which not only talks about world-class conduct but puts it into action. Technological advances will continue to speed up change and force it on us with a resultant major influence on our behaviour. Global competitiveness is primed up by the 20–40–40 formula at business enterprise or national level. It means 20 per cent of global competitiveness comes from the comparative advantage with which the nation is endowed. This could be agrarian based, minerals or any other resource. The next generator of competitiveness of 40 per cent comes from people skills and the last 40 per cent represents technological input. An earlier examination of various countries across the continent revealed an abundance of natural resources and the presence of hard-working people with the resolution to succeed. Therefore, the 20 and 40 components of the formula are already present to some extent. It is the last 40 per cent of technology which has to be built up to competitive levels. The new century will probably urge Africa to emulate post-war Japan and mount a strategy of copying technology within the confines of intellectual property rights laws. This will boost the global competitiveness of the continent significantly. More so, it will heighten a greater sense of urgency in the people, which will improve service orientation all round.

One final prognosis for the political pattern of the next century. While we advocate for democracy and transparency to reign in the new millennium, we do not want the American type of ultra-openness which ends up being tantamount to seeking perfection in an imperfect world. Africa will need to define its own version of democracy which takes into account its special circumstances. It will need to be a special blend of the traditional benevolent dictatorship and Western transparency and accountability. Our society needs to be transformed, which demands turnaround leadership strategies. By its sheer nature, a turnaround sanctions some drastic tactics to mobilise action but simultaneously share the vision with those affected. It is such political action that will enable leaders to serve their customers (the electorate) in an effective manner, as the nature of the politics will create sufficient economic growth to lift the masses from the first two rungs of Maslow's hierarchy of needs to the more exalted level of motivation.

THE BUSINESS LANDSCAPE

In the new century business should undergo as significant a transformation as the political scenario. Following the principles of less government and more self-determination of society, the business sector will need to create sufficient wealth to sustain that philosophy. More than ever before, business enterprises will need to demonstrate and deliver consistent service excellence to a new range of customers with greater demands. I see more deliberate movement from village to global economies across the land. With more openness and interdependence there will eventually be a similar economic constellation to the European Union, perhaps with a synonym such as African Commonwealth. This will go a long way towards standardising business conduct and, concomitantly, customer service across the vast region.

Of necessity, there will be more entrepreneurial leadership with a much younger age profile, driven by a less conservative investor public prepared to take risks which were previously taboo. The trend now commonplace in such industries as information technology and investment services of appointing 'yuppies' (young professionals) as executives is likely to gather momentum in the next few years. I also see a new stakeholder partnership taking root in many countries on the continent, as evidenced by such groupings as tripartite alliances of business, labour and government. In larger economies like South Africa there are considerable investments into business by trade union movements. This is a positive trend which helps bring labour stability and higher productivity in those enterprises as employees become more committed and cannot wantonly strike as it would be self-destructive.

In the horizon one can also see a decrease in social distance between boss and subordinate or employer and employee. This will be partly because of the new joint ownership of firms as discussed above and also the philosophy of joint problem solving. In some countries, again South Africa being a leading one, there are negotiated social plans between labour and employers that guide handling of business closure, retrenchment, re-skilling of employees and creation of self-employment opportunities.

The growth of smaller, informal businesses will lead to some positive developments as regards service orientation among players. First, such enterprises have the capacity to render personal service as opposed to following a standard manual in a large corporate. Second, they are compelled by business realities to be committed to total quality management and zero defect tolerance in order to attract and retain customers from large organisations. Third, it has been proved universally true that small organisations contribute more to employment creation than the big conglomerates. The most fundamental form of customer service in Africa is employment, which raises the quality of life of the employed and the extended family who depend on the breadwinner.

There is also the realistic fact of business evolution, which will see management become more of a profession than before. The proliferation of management development facilities has brought professional guidelines within the reach of many. Another push factor is the intensity of competition, which will demand more operating efficiencies, above-average customer satisfaction, greater product innovation and a consistent strategic fit of the organisation to its environment. Those ill-equipped, intuitive managers who came up through the ranks will fall short of these challenges. In fact, management will give way to leadership even at lower echelons of the organisations. Leaders have graduated from precedent-based to futuristic and pragmatic practitioners who can revel in the African winds without losing either focus or the winning streak. Furthermore, the high breed of professional leaders will display unfettered creativity, symbolic of real clock building as opposed to just the time-telling orientation of their predecessors. Lastly, that generation of leadership will place emphasis on managing information to influence the environment towards the predominance of a service culture in society. I see a new definition of an African taking root in the new millennium. In the past the reflex understanding of the word was the indigenous black whose roots have lain in Africa since time immemorial. New realities have destroyed the rigid ethnic-based definition to embrace those of other orientations whose history goes back to the last two centuries. These include some white and Asiatic people. The coloured people are naturally as African as one can be, since they are a joint product of the indigenous and the latter African. This new reality is now manifested by political parties in many countries, being inclusive of all races, which was taboo before.

This will give the new century an advantage over the past as society will be able to exploit the strengths of a more comprehensive mixture of groups. If this chemistry of unity fails, then Africa is relegated to the scrapheap because of a 'we and them' divisive racial polarisation. As a consequence, every customer in whatever form will receive only mediocre service.

LESSONS FROM THE EAST

After its defeat in World War II in the 1940s, Japan embarked on a systematic and complete national transformation. To give impetus to their economic renaissance the Japanese coupled their work ethic with good education. While in other nations young people went to North American and European universities for professional technical education and stayed there, those from Japan went back home on completion of their studies. Not only did they return with professional knowhow but also a technical propensity to improve the inventions initiated in the West. Thus they exploited the wisdom of copying success and avoided wasting resources by re-inventing the wheel. Consequently, Sony hatched the audacious goal of inventing the pocket-size transistor radio as a miniature of the large wireless model. Toyota, Mazda, Mitsubishi and other car manufacturers emerged and experienced exponential growth through understanding the emerging market customer needs and mass-producing highly durable utility vehicles at affordable prices. They also penetrated the American and other international markets. Fuji film became to Japan what Eastman Kodak was to America. Whereas in the 1950s the label 'made in Japan' carried a connotation of cheap quality, a decade later perception had shifted to seeing these products as representing quality workmanship, durability and reasonable prices. Thus, the Japanese became service heroes to a universal customer base by collectively being a learning society. Japan is one of the most populous nations in the world, yet it was possible to foster such a cult-like industrious culture. There are many lessons to be drawn from Japan that would facilitate the transformation of Africa. After all there is more commonality of cultural traits between Japanese and Africans than between African and eurocentric cultures. A few that come to mind are the specific cultural role of women, sentimental adherence to greater beings of the past and congenital humility as manifested in their courtesy and etiquette.

THE UNTOLD STORIES ABOUT AFRICA

TENACITY OF THE AFRICAN WOMAN

We observed how the Japanese work an inordinately long day without coercion and noted their dedicated togetherness in inventing or perfecting things. The African is in exactly the same league in many ways. In particular, the African woman deserves special recognition. Let us start with the traditional woman of the past. In those days her place was in the home (not the kitchen only) where she was responsible for bearing and appropriately raising children. She had to till the fields with home-made implements. Her child-bearing started as early as 13 years in some societies and went on until curbed by the menopause. Consequently, the number of children was large because of the absence of birth control. Owing to the lack of scientific medical facilities, post-natal deaths of children and the mothers were extremely common. Often today, if you ask a granny how many children she had, the answer is in two parts: three or so many died, and the survivors are so many! Children were a fundamental social security for the parents, as they would look after them in their old age, so women were under untold psychological pressure to have as many children as possible, particularly boys. It is amazing how these women balanced these demands while men were hunting or fighting.

The woes of the African woman have continued in various forms. Those based in rural areas bear the brunt of the harshness of life. The men no longer go hunting, but they go to industrial centres and towns to look for work. In the southern African region, organisations such as Wenela and Theba serve as employment bureaux for the South African mining industry, recruiting from Mozambique, Swaziland, Lesotho, Zimbabwe,

Malawi and Botswana. Even outside this mining migration the pre-dominant African way of life is that men work in towns and women stay in the rural areas to look after the home and wait for their men to come at weekends or even month-ends. This was caused by discriminatory laws that prohibited Africans from holding title deeds for property in the urban areas then designated as European land. When circumstances changed, the prices of properties rocketed, putting them out of reach of mot of the population. In the face of all this, the African woman is still symbolised by carrying a baby on her back, a bundle of firewood on her head and a bucket of water in each hand, walking home from the fields at dusk to go and start cooking for her family. This image has transcended the boundaries of time and rural setting to the modern urbanite. It is not uncommon to find a professional African woman with a large house in an urban area cooking for her family and cleaning the house herself when she can afford to hire a helper. One might ask what causes this phenomenon. The answer is simply her inborn instinct to serve others with devotion and motherly concern. This personality trait is translated directly to the customer service arena in fashion boutiques in cities, department stores, agricultural produce market stalls, flea markets and handicraft stalls on the roadside. That is the epitome of service excellence in the African woman. Indeed it is tough and hard work, but she takes it in her stride as the hallmark of womanhood is to create, build and serve. With such winners this continent can only be a winner too.

TENACITY OF THE AFRICAN MAN

'Building the Cape to Cairo railway line'

When Cecil John Rhodes, the British mining magnate and imperialist, then resident in South Africa, dreamed of constructing a railway line from the Cape of Good Hope in South Africa to Cairo in Egypt, he did not have any sophisticated machinery to do the work. Africa comprised wild virgin forests fraught with dangerous animals and crocodile-infested rivers. Yet he dreamed of a railway link across that terrain without state-of-the-art equipment. How did he intend to tame these jungles? How did he plan to build the railway line? More importantly, why did he ever think of such a railway linkage?

The easiest answer is to advance British imperialism across the continent. This is only partly true, for Rhodes was a businessman, a speculative investor and not an avowed politician (although he practised politics in the Cape) before trekking northwards to establish the roots of the federated empire of Southern and Northern Rhodesia and Nyasaland (now Zimbabwe, Zambia and Malawi respectively). Rhodes had noticed the virtues of highly industrious, faithful, obliging and helpful Africans who were a large future consumer and labour market.

Towards the turn of the nineteenth century the construction of the railway line started in South Africa and reached Zimbabwe in the early 1890s. The construction was essentially manual, undertaken by the bare hands of African men. It entailed clearing the forests, digging the parameters of the tracks, laying the heavy railway sleepers, building bridges across the rivers and carrying out all the other manual work required in construction. The labourers were of two types: those who volunteered to work for the meagre pay and conscripted labourers who would be paid a token amount at the end of the period.

This event had far-reaching social and psychological consequences. Because of the enormity of the job, absence of transport and non-existence of communication technology, these men went away from their homes for years and some never returned. Therefore, the fabric of family life was ripped apart with tragic results in some instances. My grandfather and his peer group played their part in building the railway line. The local language term then for conscription labour was 'Chibharo' (tantamount to rape) and many children born in that region were given that name by their mothers, who were left pregnant and delivered their children in the absence of husbands, who only saw them years later. This was a permanent reminder of the trauma experienced by the deserted mothers. On a positive note, the venture helped to build a social and cultural bridge across numerous tribes in the Southern and Central African region. Men were drawn from as far afield as Malawi, Zambia, Zimbabwe and Mozambique to build the railway line. Some settled in South Africa and other countries, and some South Africans settled elsewhere and became assimilated into those cultures and tribes. Intermarriages ensued which cemented relations and played the useful function of reducing inter-tribal fighting to a large extent as instinct dictates that you can't kill your in-laws.

What is the moral theme connecting Cecil John Rhodes' adventure in Africa to customer service excellence? It is simply that whilst labour conscription partly coerced some men (who could easily escape), the majority participated without being subjected to force. Yes, there was the element of meagre monetary compensation, but the fundamental motivation lay in their inherent willingness to serve others. Indeed those forefathers must be remembered with gratitude by those who now enjoy the ride on the train from Cape Town through to Victoria Falls, Harare, Zambia, Malawi and Mozambique. When one takes time to understand the arduous conditions (climatic, social and security) under which the men toiled, only then does one appreciate that it was divine commitment to service and tenacity in harsh conditions that sustained them.

SYMBOLIC DIFFERENCE OF A NAME

Further significant evidence of the service orientation of the African lies in the myth of the name of Victoria Falls on the Zambezi river bordering Zimbabwe and Zambia. In the latter half of the nineteenth century, David Livingstone, a British explorer in central Africa, arrived among the Lozi people who live along the Zambezi river. He fell sick with malaria and the villagers nursed him (probably even treated him with African medicine) until he recovered. To satisfy his inquisitiveness they carried him on a makeshift stretcher on a long journey to show him *Mosi-oya-tunya* ('the smoke that thunders'). Afterwards David Livingstone wrote to the queen of Britain advising her that he 'had discovered' the falls and named them Victoria Falls in her honour. Can you discern the vast contrast in humility and orientation towards others between the two parties? The Lozi people had lived with and known the falls for hundreds of years but had never named them Lozi Falls or any other name denoting possession or ethnic ownership. Instead they chose a neutral, descriptive name which had deep meaning as well as relevance for everyone. On the other hand, Livingstone set eyes on the falls under the guidance of the locals, but he had the temerity to claim discovery and even to name them after a queen who meant nothing to the Tonga villagers. Was it out of subservience and fear that the Lozis nursed him, fed him and ferried him to the falls? They had no obligation to this white man. Yet they assisted him in the true spirit of total service without demanding direct return payment. That is a classic example of service excellence at its highest level.

POWER OF SERVICE EXCELLENCE IN LIBERATION STRUGGLES

A number of African countries waged liberation wars to gain political freedom from their colonial masters. The practice gained momentum as the winds of political emancipation blew southwards through the continent. For example, in the first countries to become independent, mainly in West Africa, political change was achieved through negotiations which were sometimes precipitated by stone throwing and burning. By the time the movement came to Southern African countries like Angola, Mozambique, Zimbabwe and South Africa, the modus operandi had escalated to fully fledged guerrilla warfare based mainly in rural areas with occasional spill-over to the urban centres. These struggles were protracted, yet the indigenous sides were not equipped with tankers, striker planes, communication and propaganda equipment. What sustained these resistance struggles for so long with so little supportive infrastructure?

The answer lies in the network of inherent service orientation of the African people across the continent. The countries up north that were liberated first rendered assistance to those still fighting in the south. This help embraced offering refuge to guerrillas and civilians, mobilising funds and international support for arms and training, as well as international propaganda to raise support for the cause.

The liberation war in Zimbabwe lasted nearly 16 years under circumstances of unequal power on the side of freedom fighters against well-equipped Rhodesian and South African forces. First, the African spirit of togetherness could not be broken by torture or any other affliction. Each person felt duty bound to serve and save his or her compatriot in whatever way possible. That made the eliciting of counter-intelligence information by the enemy very difficult, if not impossible. Quite often when the opposition soldiers arrived at a village to extort information about the movement of the 'terrorists' they would be directed in the opposite direction in such a well-coordinated manner that it sounded credible. Second, the freedom fighters were fed with the best food from village to village for years on end. The villagers slaughtered cattle at night then walked long distances to cook and feed the fighters. Third, young boys and girls were either assigned or volunteered to become assistants to the guerrillas to boost their morale and to serve as decoys in case of detection by enemy soldiers. Fourth, able-bodied young men or women often volunteered to join the guerrillas in response to the politicisation process. In some instances, a whole school would abandon studies and cross the border into Mozambique or Zambia to undergo military training. These youngsters would be guided, fed and concealed by different villagers on this long and dangerous journey, in a well-planned subterranean manoeuvre. Fifth, every working person in town and every business person who had roots in a particular area contributed either money or clothing every month through his or her village to support the fighters. In most cases these helpers were not affluent members of the society but they willingly gave time, limited cash and belongings in the spirit of total service to one another for a noble cause. Through that service orientation little David conquered the gigantic Goliath. That is the same African spirit of service which liberated other nations such as Mozambique, Angola and lastly South Africa – indeed an amazing tale of faith in one noble vision of dignity as an African people.

FINAL REFLECTIONS

We set out to explore the philosophy of service excellence and its ramifications in relation to the effective functioning of business enterprises, government, local communities, the public service, professional disciplines, the political arena and society at large. As we defined service excellence as that level of service which far exceeds the expectations of the recipient, it follows that the concept must have a deep-rooted origin. We observed that the essence of service excellence is truly ordained by God as sustained by one of the cardinal teachings of the Lord Jesus which says 'Do unto others what you would wish to be done unto you'. The logic of this commandment is that every normal person wishes the best for him- or herself. Therefore, people should extend the same level of best treatment to those they come into contact with. Service excellence precepts are predicated upon this divine discipline which is extrapolated to the fundamentals of the generic African culture and the commercial context in order to prove the close relationship. That is the gospel of this book.

HIGHLIGHTS OF EARLIER DISCUSSION

Service excellence is a pervasive element of humanity, which is inextricably intertwined with culture. For instance, the Eurocentric culture is oriented towards social service to the needy as manifested by the missionary work done around Africa in the past two centuries, the Rotary movement, and fostering or adopting a child in need of parenthood. On the other hand, the afrocentric person is oriented towards service which has immediate results or gratification, which the eurocentric would probably ignore. This relates to helping his neighbour, supporting his extended family members, and upholding the values of the immediate environment. Service orientation is both a product and a result of culture.

Africa has some distinctive competences which give it a favourable disposition towards service excellence in many situations. Many of its constituent societies remain among those few in the world that can still perform miracles, societies which still exhibit a high level of spirituality actualised in the form of service to those in need. Example are the ancestral spirits and trances on the traditional side and the proliferation of the various sects of the Apostolic Faith whose prophets pray for the healing of the people in need. The continent has its firm comparative advantages such as the rain forests in equatorial Africa, the many big waterfalls, the pyramids of Egypt, the slave shipping points on the west African coast and the mysterious pools on top of mountains with mermaids. In most cases entry to these centres of attraction is free in the true service spirit of African togetherness.

Political stability and a measure of democracy are prerequisites for economic prosperity, which in turn influences service levels. The need for optimal economic performance of individuals, communities, societies and nations has a direct cause-effect relationship with service dispensation. An equation framework was mapped out in which the government should design an environment conducive to social growth and wealth creation; the private sector then becomes the impetus for priming the national economic engine; quasi-government institutions should safeguard dispensing of national essential services; and the informal sector should fill the service gaps created by corporate giants who cannot meet small customer needs that do not lend themselves to economies of scale benefits.

Now is the time for Africa to move out of the dependency syndrome into a self-sustenance mode. Even a Shakespearean motivation was invoked by citing that 'On such a full sea are we now afloat, / and we must take the current while it serves ...' For this to be realised, a concoction of tactics are necessary, embracing an entrepreneurial spirit among all, global competitiveness, service acculturation at every stage of our lives, an international attitude, good governance and the emulation of success stories from our continent.

WAY FORWARD

Let us conclude by re-emphasising that service excellence is about eliciting the 'wow effect' from those who receive service beyond their expectations. The whole is greater than the total sum of its parts. Africans are naturally predisposed to teamwork through their culture of communalism, villagism and togetherness, which is so deeply anchored in the fabric of the society. That distinctive African feature should constitute the nexus of the African dream. The law of incrementalism is certainly in our favour, which enables the little that each person does towards service excellence to add to a greater aggregate contributed by a whole society. The dream should constitute the world class formula of thinking globally from the humble position derived from the distinctive competence of the African people.

LONG LIVE THE AFRICAN DREAM!

Concluding remarks

In this book I endeavoured to walk a journey with you, across as much of Africa as possible to provoke a new attitude about the great continent. We shared the positives and the negatives to strike a healthy balance of perception. My objective was to create a body of interesting observations which will build a new reality of customer service as a primer for a different societal approach on this continent. This objective will have been achieved if, after reading this book; a visitor to Africa becomes wiser, a student of management learns some few tips, an employee in any capacity gains a new service orientation and the business person of any size begins to challenge their established service habits. Despite the good, the bad and the ugly revealed herein, I still remain a proud and avowed African!

Thank you for sharing the excitement with me through your readership support.

Bibliographical notes

Charlton, G 1993. *'Leadership': the human race*. Cape Town: Juta & Co.

Carlzon, J 1987. *Moments of truth*. New York: Harper & Row.

Collins, J & Porras, J 1994. *Built to last*. New York: Harper Business.

Garratt, B 1996. *The fish rots from the head*. London: HarperCollins.

Hellriegel, D & Slocum, J 1986. *Management*. California, Addison-Wesley.

Hopson, B & Scally, M 1989. *12 steps to success through service*. Oxon: Lifeskills.

Love, J 1986. *McDonald's: behind the golden arches*, NY: Bantam.

Mbeki, Thabo 1998. *Africa the time has come*. Cape Town: Tafelberg/ Mafube.

Museveni, Y 1988. *Sowing the mustard seed*. London: Cambridge University Press.